THE *healing* TOUCH OF *Jesus*

GOD'S
PASSION AND POWER
TO MAKE YOU WHOLE

THE *healing* TOUCH OF *Jesus*

DR. RICHARD LEE

HOWARD
PUBLISHING CO.

Our purpose at Howard Publishing is to:

- *Increase faith* in the hearts of growing Christians
- *Inspire holiness* in the lives of believers
- *Instill hope* in the hearts of struggling people everywhere

Because He's coming again!

Published by Howard Publishing Co., Inc.,
3117 North 7th Street, West Monroe, Louisiana 71291-2227

00 01 02 03 04 05 06 07 08 09   10 9 8 7 6 5 4 3 2 1

Library of Congress Cataloging-in-Publication Data

Lee, Richard, 1946-
     The healing touch of Jesus / Richard Lee.
          p. cm.
     ISBN 1-58229-126-8
          1. Healing—Religious aspects—Christianity. 2. Spiritual healing. I. Title.

BT732.5 .L365 2000
234'.131—dc21

                                                       00-033534

Edited by Philis Boultinghouse
Interior design by Stephanie Denney

❖

LOVINGLY DEDICATED TO

Judy Lee,

FAITHFUL WIFE AND

PRECIOUS GIFT

FROM GOD TO MY LIFE.

❖

CONTENTS

CONTENTS

❖

viii

THERE'S HOPE FOR YOUR HEALING

Do you know anyone who needs healing? Certainly you do. It is unrealistic to think that anyone could go through life and not be hurt by the cruelties of this world. Physically, mentally, emotionally, and spiritually, healing and the need for healing will always be a part of our lives. So where do we go and to whom do we turn for the healing touch we so desperately need?

Many have placed their hope in the numerous self-help books and seminars that endlessly flood our bookstores and television sets. Others have turned to religious leaders that often offer expectations that they are unable to fulfill, leaving their followers discouraged, dismayed, and often even out-of-sorts with God.

Those who study the coming trends among Americans

❖

are predicting that the first decade of this millennium, the most pressing concerns will be in the area of individual health—health for the soul, mind, and body. With that timely information, a vast number of organizations and businesses are busy creating new types of treatment centers, spas, resorts, and even Christian ministries to satisfy this thirst for health and well-being.

This book is for people who hunger for a healing they have yet to find. It's all based on the time-honored principle that Jesus wants you to be made whole. When Jesus is excluded from the mending equation, real healing just doesn't happen. Don't believe those who would tell you that time heals all wounds. Time doesn't heal all wounds. It really doesn't heal any wounds. That's a delusion. As time goes on, the *discernment* of pain merely diminishes. New experiences drive the harmful memories deeper into the recesses of our minds, where they linger until they are driven back to the surface to undermine us yet again. Unless these wounds are truly healed and cast into the depths of the ocean, they will only haunt us again. Until we get to the core of what is really hurting us and properly resolve it, these suppressed feelings will return at the worst possible moments. It may take only a cutting word or an untimely event to cause the hurt to surface and affect our whole well-being.

Pain that has gone unhealed can fuel alcohol abuse, spousal abuse, overeating, codependency, work addiction, perfectionism, and other compulsions, causing emotional and physical breakdowns of our bodies. It eventually pollutes the very things we care about most: our loved ones, our work, our friendships, and our health and prosperity. Unhealed wounds are the unseen enemies of the soul that provoke most of our suffering and failures.

This book was written to let you know how much God loves you and wants you to be complete, healthy, unbroken, and whole. If you want to know what made you the way you are and how to permanently improve your life, then this book is for you.

This book is a healing journal. It is intended to be an interactive guide. If you merely read it once and put it down never to refer to it again, it will not have fulfilled its purpose. You must cooperate with God in healing. Healing requires more than information: It requires transformation, and that takes effort. It takes an effort to get to know the One who is in the transforming business. In this book, we will journey into Scripture and learn the principles God has established through his Son, Jesus Christ, for our lives. We will learn positive steps we can take to gain God's healing. We will look at our suffering and discover how God desires to use it for our growth and his glory. You will be encouraged and uplifted with the truth of God's Word and the incredible healing power he offers to each and every one of us if we only embrace his healing touch in our lives.

*E*ven though I walk
through the valley of
the shadow of death,
I will fear no evil,
for you are with me;
your rod and your staff,
they comfort me.

—Psalm 23:4

Chapter One

WHERE IS JESUS WHEN I NEED HIM MOST?
You Can Be Made Whole

Not long ago I received a letter from one of the listeners to our broadcast. It read:

Dear Pastor Lee,

I am very discouraged and downhearted at this time. I'm a middle-aged man who is in good health. Because of problems in my field of work, I've been unemployed for many months now. I can get no unemployment compensation. My wife has been sick for a long time, and it is evident she will never work again. I need a job. I want a job that will support us, but it's just not there. Often I think of suicide, but I believe that is wrong. I pray and I try, but nothing seems to happen. Where is God, Pastor? I've been a Christian for forty years, but I see no light at the end of my tunnel. Pastor, please tell me, where is God when I need him the most?

Pain and suffering are realities of life. They stretch our faith and test the limits of our endurance. More than anything else, they often push us to the very brink of personal disaster. Some of us have given up on life because of the pain of human suffering. Our hearts cry out for help, hope, and healing.

"Where is God?" we ask.

"Can he help me?" we cry.

"Does he care?" we wonder.

These are normal questions for people in pain— whether physical, spiritual, or emotional. We all want to know if God is great enough to help us or kind enough to care about our suffering. Something deep within us cries out to God. It is as though the human heart knows that only God can help us in such times of distress. Our pain drives us to the only One who can help us. No matter what our religious background or spiritual condition, the cry of our hurting hearts is the cry for God to intervene in our lives. How many times have you heard someone cry out, "Oh, God!" in a moment of personal anguish? There are no real atheists in times of personal crises. Even the hardest hearts become tenderized by human pain and suffering.

WHERE IS JESUS WHEN YOU NEED HIM MOST?

Where is Jesus when you can't take the problems of life anymore and your faith seems to be at an end? I have to admit that I've asked that question myself. Most everyone asks it sooner or later. Whether it be a category-three tornado that rips through an Oklahoma town shattering the lives of countless people or a lone gunman who enters a Baptist church in Fort Worth, Texas, killing seven people and injuring seven others before he takes his own life or any of a hundred other scenarios, disaster comes to us: It shakes our belief system and fills us with fear; it makes us question our very faith in God.

Things can go wrong even when we are doing everything we can to live a life that is right in the sight of God. The truth is that bad things do happen to good people. But the question is, Where is Jesus in the middle of my problems? The answer is in the question. Jesus is right where he said he would be—right in the middle of your problems.

Jesus was there in the midst of the pain at Wedgwood Baptist Church. Satan's attempts to hurt that church and those people were curbed by God's intervention. God directed the teachers of the children's classes and preschool classes to run late so that they would not be in the playground when the gunman walked past it. He pulled the bottom off of the pipe bomb that was thrown into the crowd but never exploded. He directed a young girl with scoliosis to shield a disabled friend with her body, while directing the bullet away from major organs, because of the curve in her spine, saving her life. He directed the 911 call to come in on a police radio, so emergency vehicles could be dispatched immediately, without spending precious time to verify that that call was real.

Jesus also led the United Methodist church to send fifteen people the following Sunday to cover the childcare. He led people in another church to drive five hours just so they could march around the church and pray during the Sunday morning services. Jesus used this tragedy to reach millions of people around the world through the live international CNN broadcast of the funeral. Jesus was right in the middle of their pain.

Jesus Never Takes a Time-Out

Jesus is never absent from our troubles. He takes no time-outs. He is always ready to help us handle our problems. The apostle Paul would say that Jesus "comforts us in all our troubles" (2 Corinthians 1:4). But there is no place in the Bible that says he will keep us from trouble. It can be difficult to accept troubles if we think of Jesus as a friend who will lead us through life unscathed, steering us clear of any danger.

King David came to grips with this truth when he wrote: "Even though I walk through the valley of the shadow of death, I will fear no evil, for you are with me; your rod and your staff, they comfort me" (Psalm 23:4). David had to rely on that truth years later when his own son threatened his life. Absalom wanted to take over his father's kingdom. He had gathered an army and prepared to attack the king's forces. When David learned of this, he knew that victory meant saving his empire but could also mean losing Absalom, so he ordered his forces to spare his son's life. Later, his generals reported the good news that his kingdom was saved; however, they also had to bear the bad news that

Absalom had died in a freak accident when his charging horse carried him into a low-limbed tree that broke his neck and took his life.

Reading Psalm 23, we are brought face to face with a man coming to grips with the pain of life and the peace of knowing that God would shepherd him through this and every valley of life.

JESUS SHARES OUR SUFFERING WITH US

No one enjoys being hurt physically or emotionally. However, no matter how much we seek to protect ourselves and our loved ones from difficult life situations, we still remain susceptible to pain. The fact that Jesus would come to this earth as the incarnate Son of God shows his willingness to share our suffering, our troubles, and our pain. God demonstrates to us, through his Son, that his love for us does not preclude disaster but instead drives him to suffer the disaster with us. Jesus' suffering on the cross transcended human suffering—for he bore not only the physical pain but the sins of the world. This was the ultimate demonstration of his love for us—a love that would cause him to reach out to comfort a man who was crucified alongside him and say, "Today you will be with me in paradise" (Luke 23:43). This same love compelled him to look down at a grieving mother and say, " 'Dear woman, here is your son,' and to the disciple [the apostle John], 'Here is your mother.' From that time on, this disciple took her into his home" (John 19:26–27).

If Jesus could share the suffering of others while suffering

❖

the weight of the sins of the world upon his shoulders, certainly he can share your sufferings, no matter what they may be. In fact, it is through suffering that we can truly encounter Christ. It is a great comfort to know that in our suffering, Christ also suffers with us. Suffering affords possibilities for growth that better times do not. As you come to see hurt as a unique opportunity to encounter the healing touch of grace from Jesus, you are able to move from a position of distress and depression to one of acceptance and victory.

JESUS GIVES US HOPE IN OUR SUFFERING

> Jesus left there and went along the Sea of Galilee. Then he went up on a mountainside and sat down. Great crowds came to him, bringing the lame, the blind, the crippled, the mute and many others, and laid them at his feet; and he healed them. The people were amazed when they saw the mute speaking, the crippled made well, the lame walking and the blind seeing. And they praised the God of Israel. (Matthew 15:29–31)

In this passage Jesus did a lot more than physical healing— he brought hope. A father whose daughter had just died had no hope. A woman who had been bleeding for twelve long years had no hope. Men who were blind and couldn't work or be independent had no hope. A person who couldn't communicate through speech knew only frustration, not hope.

But Jesus brought hope. He raised the dead and stopped the bleeding; he gave sight to the blind and voice to the mute. And Jesus brings us hope too. We know that we can't do what we need to do to please God. Even the apostle Paul writes about his frustration and hopelessness before his own sin (see Romans 7:15–24). But into the picture of hopelessness, Jesus brings hope. He brings hope through his sacrifice for our sins. He brings hope by sharing eternal life with his followers. He gives us hope by personally bringing us the promises of God.

Jesus says something very important to us through his healing miracles. He reminds us that when he is with us, we always have hope. And we do.

God Provides Answers in His Word

If you really want to find God's answers to your troubles, turn to his Word. The Bible is filled with principles for living, and in it we find the answers to the questions that so often trouble our souls. Finding the healing touch of Jesus is not a vague, mystical experience. Rather, it is the result of a deliberate search for truth in his revealed Word.

Jesus is always with us. Even in our darkest hour, he is at work in our lives. We simply need to learn to discern his healing touch.

Surely the arm of the Lord is not too
    short to save,
    nor his ear to dull to hear.
But your iniquities have separated
    you from your God;
your sins have hidden his face from you,
    so that he will not hear.

—*Isaiah 59:1–2*

Chapter Two

WHY CAN'T I FIND GOD'S HEALING?
Four Hindrances to Wholeness

In the Gospel of Mark, we see an interesting picture. Jesus has just called Matthew, a Jewish tax collector, to be his disciple. Now, Matthew was not at all popular among the Jews. He was, in fact, seen as a traitor. He served the Romans and collected money from his own people (while extorting money from them as well). After Jesus called Matthew, Jesus went to his house and had a meal with none other than tax collectors, publicans, and sinners. When the scribes and Pharisees saw this, they began to complain, "How can Jesus eat with these sinners?" Jesus' response was not what they expected. "It is not the healthy who need a doctor, but the sick. I have not come to call the righteous, but sinners" (2:17).

Time after time we see in the Bible that Jesus desires for all to be made whole. Being whole means to be complete, to be full of health, to live a life of full abundance in our whole being. This includes our body, our soul, and our spirit. In fact, Jesus said that the reason he came to this earth was "to seek and to save what was lost" (Luke 19:10) and that we "may have life, and have it to the full" (John 10:10). His plan and purpose for us is that we be complete, undiminished, unbroken, and whole.

Throughout his ministry, we see him healing the sick and hurting. He had compassion on those who were not whole, and with his mighty touch, he restored them.

While in Jerusalem, Jesus came to the pool of Bethesda (incidentally, *Bethesda* means "House of Grace"), where many were waiting to be healed. "At certain seasons" (John 5:4 NASB), an angel would stir the waters, and the first to enter the waters would be healed of his or her disease, no matter what it was. One man had been there for thirty-eight years—since before Christ had been born.

Jesus came to him and asked him a simple question: "Do you desire to be made whole?" (John 5:6 MKJV). The man answered that he had no one to help him into the water and that others always entered before him so he could not be healed. Jesus said to him, "Get up! Pick up your mat and walk."

Jesus approaches us today and asks us the same simple question: "*Do you want to be made whole?*" If it's true that he desires wholeness for us, then why are so many not whole?

Why are so many unhappy and unfulfilled? Why are so many filled with pain? Part of the answer lies in our own lack of understanding. Many are unaware of the hindrances to wholeness.

⌒HINDRANCE #1:
WE IGNORE THE LAWS OF SOWING AND REAPING

Perhaps the first way we hinder our wholeness is by ignoring the laws of sowing and reaping. Galatians 6:7 says, "Do not be deceived: God cannot be mocked. A man reaps what he sows." Second Corinthians 9:6 goes further to explain this law: "Whoever sows sparingly will also reap sparingly, and whoever sows generously will also reap generously." Not only do we reap what we sow, but we reap in proportion to what we sow. Genesis 8:22 says, "As long as the earth endures, seedtime and harvest...will never cease."

Even the Book of Ecclesiastes says, "A time to plant and a time to uproot" (3:2). We live in a universe of stimulus and response. In fact, Newton's third law of motion states that for every action, there is an opposite and equal reaction. God made it that way. There are three laws of reaping and sowing:

1. You reap what you sow.
2. You reap more than you sow.
3. You reap later than you sow.

We begin to see that God's *promises are often preceded by our action.* God often asks something from us before he gives us what he wants us to have. Examples of this are many, but here are just a few.

1. We repent of our sins—he forgives us.
2. We yield to his lordship—he watches over and directs our lives.
3. We yield to him our faith, family, and finances—he blesses us!

We must also understand that only what we give him can be multiplied back to us. If we give nothing, he has nothing to multiply! Remember—it is the law of "sowing and reaping," not the law of "reaping and sowing." So often we approach God with our hand out and say, "God, if you will give me this, then I will give back to you." But in God's economy, that is not the way it works. When we neglect the opportunity to give, we reject the opportunity to receive. It is the principle of reciprocity.

HINDRANCE #2:
WE LIMIT THE WAYS OF GOD

We also hinder our wholeness by limiting God. When my daughter was a child, learning the books of the Old Testament, she could say every book correctly until she came to the Book of Lamentations. She would always say "Limitations." Of course, her mother and I thought it was cute, but we also saw that it carried a profound insight. So many believers live life as a book of limitations. But for the child of God who walks by faith, life is a book of possibilities. I like this poem:

Faith, mighty faith, the Christian sees
And looks to God alone.
He laughs at life's impossibilities
And cries, "It shall be done!"

So often we try to give God the agenda. We tell him what to do, how to do it, and when it should be done. Fortunately, more often than not, God does not follow our advice. In fact, God rarely does things the way we expect them to be done! In Isaiah 55:8–9, God declares, "For my thoughts are not your thoughts, neither are your ways my ways.... As the heavens are higher than the earth, so are my ways higher than your ways and my thoughts than your thoughts." Simply put, God doesn't think like we think, so we should not place him into our bottle of how he should do things. We should instead call to him, and when we do, he promises, "I will answer you and tell you great and unsearchable things you do not know" (Jeremiah 33:3). This makes life exciting and adventuresome because we know that if we are faithful to God, he will provide what we need in his way and in his time. He has never failed to do just that, and he never will.

A humorous story is told of an old woman who lived by the side of the road in a very small house. It was a meager residence with merely a tin roof for covering. One day she had no flour in her house to make bread, so she began praying on her front porch for God to provide. It just so happened that two mean little boys were walking by and heard her. One said to the other, "Let's go down to the store and buy a bag of flour and fool that old woman." They agreed and rushed down to the store and bought a bag of flour. They hurried back and found the woman still in prayer. They proceeded to climb onto the back of the house and roll the bag of flour down the front of the tin roof until it fell with a thud to the ground. This startled the woman from her prayers, and when she realized what it was, she began to shout and praise God for his provision. The boys began mocking her and laughing, shouting from the rooftop. "Foolish woman, God didn't give you that flour. We did." Wisely, the woman shouted back to them, "Yes, boys, God sent me the flour, even though he had to use two little demons to deliver it." In my own life, God has often chosen to meet my needs by using the most unusual people in the most unpredictable ways.

We should never limit the way God chooses to work, and we should be quick to recognize his provision—even when it comes in an unexpected way.

*H*INDRANCE #3:
WE TALK FAITHLESS TALK

Next, we hinder wholeness by talking faithless talk. Proverbs says that "as he thinks in his heart, so is he" (23:7 NKJV). And Jesus said, "Out of the abundance of the heart the mouth speaks" (Matthew 12:34 NKJV). Negative and faithless talk will destroy your belief. It will cast a shadow on all of your life, eventually bringing you down into the valley of fear and doubt. Negative words can make sunshine seem like rain, joy seem like sorrow, and happiness seem like pain. Jesus draws a strong correlation between what we say and what we do. He told a Roman centurion who begged for his daughter to be healed, "As thou hast believed, so be it done unto thee" (Matthew 8:13 KJV). In fact, many times in the Scriptures, Jesus said it was people's faith that healed them. Even in salvation, he has instructed us that we must confess with our mouths and believe in our hearts (see Romans 10:9). Faithless talk always produces a faithless walk.

☙ HINDRANCE #4:
WE LIVE WITH BROKEN VOWS

The final thing that hinders our wholeness is living with broken vows. Most of us have made vows to God in one way or another. We may have found ourselves in trouble and cried out, "God, I'll give you my life if you will just help me out of this one." Or when one of our children is sick, we vow, "God, I'll serve you forever if you will just allow my child to get well." Or we hit financial difficulties and promise, "God, if you will help me with this, I'll honor you with tithes and offerings." It was once said that there are no atheists in fox-holes. We make promises and vows to God when we are in trouble. Unfortunately, when the trouble subsides, we tend to forget them, but God doesn't! God takes the vows we make to him very seriously. He expects and desires that we follow through on our promises.

The whole Book of Jonah is devoted to this very subject. It is about one man's vow to God and what God did to make sure he kept it. God came and spoke to his servant Jonah, saying, "Go to the great city of Nineveh and preach against it, because its wickedness has come up before me" (1:2). Jonah knew that he had made a commitment to God and that he was called to be his prophet, but he also knew that his was not an easy task. The Ninevites were known for their cruelty, and they especially hated the Jews. Jonah was most likely afraid. But he also knew that God would be merciful to the Ninevites if they repented, and he didn't want them to be spared. Jonah hated the Ninevites as much as they hated the Jews.

So Jonah hopped on a boat and tried to run from the oath he had made to God. But a great storm came while he was at sea, and Jonah knew that God was punishing him. So he told the sailors to throw him overboard so that at least they would be spared. Jonah was swallowed by a giant fish and spent three days in its belly praying. He finally prayed, "What I have vowed I will make good" (2:9). Jonah was spewed up onto dry ground, and he paid the debt he vowed.

God always wants what is best for us, but we must be prepared to fulfill our commitment. Jonah broke his vow to God, and it cost him dearly. The Book of Proverbs warns us: "It is a trap for a man to dedicate something rashly and only later to consider his vows" (20:25).

So what do we do with broken vows? First, we must go back and remember our vows. Then, we must acknowledge them before the Lord. We must ask his forgiveness and commit to fulfilling the vows we have made to him.

Have you made vows to God that you have failed to keep? Promises that have gone unfulfilled? If so, take time to fulfill those vows and get that hindrance out of the way so that God can work on your behalf.

❖

If there is one thing that is certain, it is the fact that God desires his children to be whole, complete, and fulfilled. But first, we must rid ourselves of those hindrances that keep us from these blessings. Simply put, only when we cooperate with God and by faith position ourselves in right relationship with him are we able to find the healing touch we so desire and he desires to give us. The principle taught by the psalmist is still true today: "No good thing does he withhold from those whose walk is blameless" (Psalm 84:11).

$\mathscr{S}$urely he took up our infirmities
　　and carried our sorrows,
yet we considered him stricken by God,
　　smitten by him, and afflicted.
But he was pierced for our transgressions,
　　he was crushed for our iniquities;
the punishment that brought us peace was
　　　upon him,
　　and by his wounds we are healed.

—*Isaiah 53:4–5*

Chapter Three

WHAT DO I DO WITH THE PAIN?

Finding Emotional Healing

Before we get into the details of Jesus' healing touch, we need to clearly understand that complete healing is possible. Often we see Christ's work of salvation only in terms of forgiveness from our sins. But salvation is much more than this. Jesus came to heal us from all our wounds and set us free from all that binds us. Yes, hurt is inevitable, but healing is possible. Jesus Christ calls us to be whole and makes this possible through his willingness to be broken for us.

Too often we take a fatalistic view about the damaging effects of tragedy. We may feel bitterness and anger as a result of tragedy but at the same time feel "I am what I am because of what has happened to me, and there is nothing I can do about it now." Yes, life experiences do involve hurt and emotional injury. But that is not the final word on the matter. Just because I experience hurt from the hands of others or natural causes doesn't mean I have to go through life an emotional cripple in bondage to the pain and anger associated with those hurts.

Many people continue to live in slavery to the past. Some lack the faith to believe that Jesus can set them free from the gripping effects of their hurts. Some are not ready to forgive those who hurt them and are resolved to cling to their anger and the pain that is associated with it. Others might be ready to forgive and may have even tried to forgive, but they can't get any relief from the anger and pain. Still others are simply afraid of experiencing more pain and, knowing that healing will involve more pain, would rather remain stuck in park.

Three steps are necessary for emotional healing:

1. Accept the gain that comes from pain.
2. Allow the compassionate Christ to share your burden.
3. Release the anger through forgiveness.

STEP #1:
ACCEPT THE GAIN THAT COMES FROM PAIN

From Toledo, Ohio, comes the story of a little girl named Beverly Smith. It seems Beverly was a strange sort of child because she never cried when she got hurt. At first, her parents thought she was just unusually brave, but after a while, they became concerned. It seemed that nothing that ever happened to Beverly made her cry.

Finally, after taking Beverly to a doctor, it was discovered that she had a rare disease of the nervous system that prevented her from feeling pain.

The doctors cautioned Mrs. Smith that as long as Beverly lived, she could not be left alone, for she could be gravely injured and never feel the pain. So we see that physical pain is often a blessing in disguise.

God often uses the worst circumstances to bring about the best results in our lives. He allows us to experience pain, sorrow, anguish, and disappointment so that we might reach out to him and find his grace sufficient to meet our needs. When everything is going well in our lives, it is easy to forget God. Pain is the great reminder that we can't make it without him.

God also uses pain to remind us of what is really important in life. It is easy to focus on the blessings of God and forget that he is the source of those blessings. We can get so caught up in the blessings that we forget the One who blesses us. We can get so excited about the gifts he gives us that we forget the Giver of the gifts.

Most of all, God uses pain and suffering to display his power and grace. When we struggle with the difficulties of life, we recognize afresh how great his provisions really are on our behalf. Most of our problems, difficulties, and pains are only temporary. They get our attention focused on God

❖

so that he can heal us, strengthen our faith, and restore us to even more effective lives in serving him.

Sometimes, in order for healing to take place, we have to revisit the original pain and face it again. For some, it is easier to forget it and put it away in a deep recess of the mind than to deal with it.

A pastor friend of mine broke his finger but never had it reset. Consequently, it healed crooked, and today he can't make a tight fist. He was advised that for his finger to straighten out, it would have to be rebroken. Many people avoid going to their physicians to relieve an ailment because they know that to do so will require more pain. The bottom line is simple: Physical healing sometimes requires more pain.

Everyone has his or her own way of coping with pain. Some go to a friend, some use spiritual resources such as prayer and Bible reading, some lose themselves in their work, while others cope with the hurt through some form of entertainment. While these are good ways to deal with the pain, there is a danger of immersing yourself in them in order to hide the hurt and not deal with it.

Just like physical healing, emotional healing, if it is to be complete enough to address the deepest part of our injury, may also involve a second experience of pain. But the second experience is not like the first. The first experience probably hit you like a ton of bricks; you may have felt out of control and were likely unable to process the pain in a healthy way. But revisiting the pain for the purpose of healing is a different matter. The second time around is by choice and brings understanding and cleansing.

All hurt involves loss, and for emotional healing to take place, we must often allow ourselves to face again all the feelings associated with that loss, uproot these hidden hurts, see them in the light of God's mercy toward us, release them to him, and go on with living.

$\mathscr{S}$TEP #2:
ALLOW THE COMPASSIONATE CHRIST TO SHARE YOUR BURDEN

Although the hurt you feel inside will often cause you to want to go into a corner and hide, there is something inside that cries out for love. It is within our human nature to want to share our hurt with someone who can care for, support, and love us.

Jesus is the ultimate burden bearer. Isaiah described this attribute of Christ when he penned these words: "Surely he took up our infirmities and carried our sorrows, yet we considered him stricken by God, smitten by him, and afflicted. But he was pierced for our transgressions, he was crushed for our iniquities; the punishment that brought us peace was upon him, and by his wounds we are healed" (53:4–5). God became personally involved with our hurts when he sent his Son to be the one who would bear our burdens, carry our sorrows, take upon himself our sickness and infirmities, and heal us.

Because Jesus came to this earth and suffered with us and for us, he understands our suffering and is able to share our burdens. This suffering qualifies him to help us when we can't take the hurt anymore. When we feel like throwing in the towel because of hurts, disappointments, or losses, we need to remember that Jesus is always available to share these burdens, and he shares them with *compassion*.

Three days came and went while Jesus healed the sick brought to him on that hillside in Galilee. A crowd of four thousand men, not counting women and children, had followed Jesus to a lonely place away from the towns. Jesus had compassion on the crowd, called his disciples together, and said, "I do not want to send [the people] away hungry, or they may collapse on the way" (Matthew 15:32). He then proceeded to feed the entire crowd with only seven loaves of bread and a few fish.

In itself, this is an amazing story—a miracle! But we would be wrong to see it as the whole story. If today, two thousand years after the event, we were to read this story out of context, it would be of little or no significance. The full story is not the story of the God-man named Jesus who miraculously fed thousands of people many centuries ago. The real story—the "story behind the story," as the journalists say—is about a man who healed lepers, a man who caused the blind to see and the deaf to hear, a man who brought dead people back to life, a man who welcomed sinners into his company and forgave them their sins, a man who suffered and died for us human beings, a man with total respect and reverence for all people as God's supreme miracle of creation. The real story in this miracle and in all the miracle stories about Jesus is that he cared enough to do what he did for other people. He cared for them one person at a time. Each with special needs for healing. He listened to them and then he healed them.

During the first two decades of the twentieth century, a great number of babies less than one year of age wasted away in hospitals and children's institutions and died from unknown causes. In some institutions it was customary to describe the condition of all seriously sick infants as "hopeless" on admission cards. Among the doctors who were confronted with infant mortality every day was Dr. Fritz Talbot of the Children's Clinic in Dusseldorf, Germany. Dr. Talbot had uncommon success in dealing with sick children. As he made his rounds, he would be followed from ward to ward by groups of interns seeking new ways of handling children's diseases. One such intern was Dr. Joseph Brennermann, who told this story:

> Many times we would come across a child for whom everything had failed. For some reason the child was hopelessly wasting away. When this would happen, Dr. Talbot would take the child's chart and scrawl some indecipherable prescription on it. In most of the cases, the magic formula took effect and the child began to prosper. My curiosity was aroused, and I wondered if the famous doctor had developed some new type of wonder drug. One day, after rounds, I returned to the ward and tried to decipher Dr. Talbot's scrawl. I had no luck, and so I turned to the head nurse and asked her what the prescription was. "Old Anna," she said. Then she pointed to a grandmotherly woman seated in a large rocker with a baby on her lap. "Whenever we have a baby for whom everything we could

do has failed, we turn the child over to Old Anna. She has more success than all the doctors and nurses in this institution combined."[1]

In most infant-care centers today, one of the most important pieces of equipment is a rocking chair. Compassionate, tender care is a great healer.

Sometimes sharing our burdens with Jesus is God's way of preparing us to share them with others. God often shows his love to us through the compassion of others. Sometimes, all that is needed is a listener with a face and gentle arms to hug.

When you allow yourself to experience the pain again and allow Jesus to share your burden, then you are ready to take your next step toward total healing.

STEP #3:
RELEASE THE ANGER THROUGH FORGIVENESS

In the sixth chapter of Matthew, Jesus teaches his disciples how to pray through what is commonly known as "The Lord's Prayer." This is the most important prayer recorded in all of Scripture, because it serves as a model prayer for all Christians. There are six petitions within this prayer, but Jesus elaborates on only one of them. It is not the petition for the kingdom of God to come to earth or the request for our daily bread, but his plea that God forgive us our debts as we forgive our debtors. Perhaps he returned to this petition because it is so foreign to human nature to forgive. Without a doubt, he felt it needed an explanation and even a warning to those who chose to neglect it.

Christ expounds on this petition in verses 14 and 15 when he says, "For if you forgive men when they sin against you, your heavenly Father will also forgive you. But if you do not forgive men their sins, your Father will not forgive your sins." Notice, we must forgive men their sins against us if God is going to forgive our sins. Not that God forgives only on an exchange basis, but this teaching clearly indicates that our forgiveness of others is a necessary part of God's forgiveness to us.

Christ places a high importance on our forgiveness of others. It is not an option, but a command. Why is this so important? Why must we forgive? Scripture gives us several reasons.

REFUSAL TO FORGIVE HARMS OUR ENTIRE BEING

Unforgiveness is a spiritual sickness that affects our entire being—body, soul, and spirit. The greatest spiritual sickness is the sickness of unforgiveness. Its roots run deep into our very souls. One root may be anger, another hatred, one bitterness, and another resentment. Not only do these roots run deep, but they will also torment our souls and sap the very energy of happiness from our lives. When this happens, we become our own greatest enemy. We become out of control and unable to maintain a relationship with the Father.

If we have unforgiving hearts, it will be impossible for us to live effective Christian lives. A lack of forgiveness is often indicative of a deep-seated bitterness that robs the soul of vitality. The great problem with bitterness is that it spreads like a plague until it affects every relationship in our lives.

Once we look at life through the eyes of bitterness, we will never see it in proper focus or perspective. And if we don't get over this bitterness, we will never be able to trust anyone again.

There is a Greek legend of a man who had been tormented all of his life by a strange, veiled figure. No matter what he did, it seemed that this figure would haunt him and take away everything that he ever had. Each time he would eat, as he would bring the food to his mouth, this veiled figure would appear and snatch it away. Every time he would strive to succeed and gain happiness, the veiled figure would appear and take it all away. Finally, when he felt he could stand it no more, he decided in his heart that he would unveil his tormentor and put him to death. So he waited for the perfect moment and when it came, he reached up and ripped off the mask from his enemy's face. In shock and dismay, he beheld the face of his enemy, and the face was his own.

Many of us are our own worst enemies. Our unforgiving spirit eats away at our spiritual vitality until we self-destruct. The Bible says, "Better a patient man than a warrior, a man who controls his temper than one who takes a city" (Proverbs 16:32). In other words, the person who can rule over himself is greater than one who can conquer a city. Self-discipline and self-control are two of the greatest assets we can develop.

Often, we create our own misery when we wallow in bitterness. Certainly, that is true when we live in unforgiveness. We can surround our souls with unforgiving spirits and block the forgiveness of God with which he desires to reach our hearts. The most sinister thing about an unforgiving spirit is that it may not hurt the person at whom it is directed, but it will destroy us.

Booker T. Washington was a famous black educator who was often criticized and maligned by his peers in the white community. They argued that he would never succeed in reaching a high standard of education or in building a quality institution. But Washington was a man who had a deep faith in Christ. He had God in his life and knew that God could overcome every obstacle before him. He said, "I will never allow any man to destroy or denigrate my soul by making me hate him."

Hatred degrades our hearts. When we allow ourselves to become consumed with hate, we will eventually become the object of our own bitterness. An unforgiving spirit can bury any one of us alive. We need to forgive in order to rid ourselves of spiritual sickness.

The Bible gives us a clear picture of how an unforgiving spirit and a vengeful grudge can lead to our own demise. In the Book of Esther, we see the story of three main characters —Haman, Mordecai, and Esther. Haman was a great man in the government of Persia. He was the prime minister under King Xerxes from 483 B.C. until about 474 B.C. Haman was a prideful man who was insulted by one man's refusal to pay him homage. "When Haman saw that Mordecai would not kneel down or pay him honor, he was enraged" (Esther 3:5).

In the Law, God commanded that the Jews not worship or bow to any person or thing but God. When Mordecai would pass by Haman, he would not bow or pay homage to Haman. This insult grew into a disdain for the entire race that Mordecai represented. "Having learned who Mordecai's people were, he scorned the idea of killing only Mordecai. Instead Haman looked for a way to destroy all of Mordecai's people, the Jews, throughout the whole kingdom of Xerxes" (v. 6). Haman hated Mordecai so much that he plotted an annihilation of the Jewish people to begin with Mordecai's hanging at the gallows.

Often, this is where prejudices take root. A person's bitterness grows like leavened bread. It cannot be contained but soon spreads to include generalities like a race or gender, age or name.

It so happened that the king's new wife, Esther, was also a Jew. When Mordecai, who had raised Esther, learned of the plot to kill the Jews, he sent word to Queen Esther and exhorted her to step forward and save her people. The queen then began looking for an opportunity to reveal the plot to the king. She decided it was safest to schedule a banquet and share the plot before his council.

Meanwhile, Haman's bitterness toward Mordecai continued to fester, and he shared his feelings with his wife and friends, looking for support and approval. At his wife's urging, he prepared a gallows seventy-five feet high on which to hang Mordecai.

We, like Haman, enjoy nursing our wounds in the presence of others and feel the need to share our "mistreat-ment." We forget that only the Father can set it right and that only the Father can heal our wounds.

King Xerxes became disturbed the night before the ban-quet. He could not sleep and requested that the daily logs of the kingdom business be read to him. In those logs, the king discovered that Mordecai had once saved his life by report-ing a plot against him. The king was so appreciative that he determined to reward Mordecai publicly for his loyalty.

The day of the banquet, before Esther had made her request, the king asked Haman how he would reward some-one who deserved honor. Haman, thinking it was himself, described elaborate gifts and recognition. In a cruel twist of fate, the king told Haman to present the honors he had described to none other than Mordecai.

At the scheduled banquet, Queen Esther took pains to set the right atmosphere for the king and his guest. She knew that her life could be in danger if she offended the king in her petition, but she also knew that her calling was to protect her people, the Jews, and that her life was in jeop-ardy if she did not do this. At the right time, after the king had enjoyed some wine, she told the king of Haman's plan to slaughter the Jews, including herself. The king was enraged at the thought and the man behind the plot. When he left the room, Haman went to Esther to beg for his life. Haman's demise was in the making. When the king returned, he interpreted Haman's gesture as a threat against his wife, Esther. He accused Haman of assault and ordered

What Do I Do with the Pain?

❖

his hanging, poetically, on the very gallows built for Mordecai.

Just like Haman, unforgiveness will hang your heart and bury your soul. It is like acid within each of us that will eat the life away from the inside out.

Refusal to Forgive Blocks Our Joy

We cannot have true joy if we have continued bitterness dwelling in our minds and hearts. Sometimes we remove hurts from our immediate consciousness but store them in the back closets of our hearts. Hurts, hatred, envy, and resentment may be forgotten by our minds, but they are often still remembered and unforgiven in our hearts. This places a barrier in our lives to prayer, keeping us from being effective in our walk with Christ. When we come across a person against whom we hold resentment, it frustrates us and keeps us from becoming the victorious Christians that Christ calls us to be. We may think that we have given them "partial" forgiveness, when in reality, there is no such thing.

A great Christian lady, Corrie ten Boom, was put in a concentration camp during World War II. Her experiences in that camp were terrible—almost beyond imagination. Her own sister died in that camp, but Corrie lived to share some of the horrible experiences she endured—particularly, how she was often stripped naked and forced to shower in front of an SS guard. This German guard constantly mocked her and made vulgar statements concerning her.

When the war was over, Corrie became a Christian

spokeswoman and carried the message of Christ's forgiveness around the world. One day, after she had spoken in Munich, she took time to address the people who had gathered to meet her. They shook her hand and told her what her message had meant to them. Eventually, a man came up to her, stuck his hand out, and said, "It's true, God's forgiveness is good, isn't it?" As she looked into his face, she recognized him to be the wicked SS guard. Immediately, as she stared back at him, she thought of the times he had humiliated her.

> I thought in my heart that I had forgiven him, but as he reached out his hand, my hand froze by my side and I could not reach out and take his. Here I was, a world famous forgiver, and I had come face to face with a man I could not touch. So I prayed to God, "God, forgive me, and my inability to forgive." When I asked God for that, he gave me the grace to reach out my hand and take his hand and say, "Yes, God is good."[2]

She learned in that moment what each of us needs to learn. Forgiveness is a matter of the heart. We must not merely forgive with our lips, but with our hearts. Only then can we live above the offenses of others and find true joy.

To forgive does not mean that the offense never comes to mind—that may be humanly impossible—but it means treating others with a sincere heart, not holding offense against them.

Refusal to Forgive Puts Us in God's Judgment Seat

Scripture teaches that it is not our place to judge. Romans 12:19 says, "Do not take revenge, my friends, but leave room for God's wrath, for it is written: 'It is mine to avenge; I will repay,' says the Lord." When we judge others and refuse to forgive, we take upon ourselves a right that God has reserved for himself. He alone can render proper judgment. We cannot possibly know all the motives, circumstances, and backgrounds of those who have hurt us. Therefore, we must be willing to forgive and leave judgment up to God.

I can remember my mother saying:

There's so much bad in the best of us
And so much good in the worst of us,
That it ill behooves any of us
To criticize the rest of us.

In Matthew 7, Christ admonishes us not to judge the sawdust in a brother's eye before removing the plank in our own. None of us is above reproach. The Bible clearly reminds us, "For all have sinned and come short of the glory of God." None of us will reach perfection this side of heaven. None of us is capable of knowing everything about everyone else. Therefore, we are incapable of rendering final judgment on any matter.

Forgiveness reminds us that we have not been given the right to judge others. In fact, our willingness to forgive is our way of trusting God to do the judging. We don't have to worry about getting even because God keeps score. We will do well to trust that he knows what he is doing. We just need to concentrate on keeping our hearts right and leave the justice up to God.

Christ gives us an amazing promise in Mark 11. He says that whatever we ask for, if we have faith and believe that we will receive it, it will be ours. First John 5:14 adds the stipulation that our request must also be within his will: "If we ask anything according to his will, he hears us." The promise of answered prayer is an amazing promise indeed. But the promise comes with a condition.

Look closely at Mark 11:25–26: "And when you stand praying, if you hold anything against anyone, forgive him, so that your Father in heaven may forgive you your sins. But if you do not forgive, neither will your Father who is in heaven forgive your sins."

Before we look at the condition, note the breadth of Christ's command: "if you hold *anything* against *anyone.*" This statement is all inclusive. "Anything" includes not only the sins of others that we might hold against them but also any personality traits we may dislike. "Anyone" includes not only our Christian brothers and sisters but all with whom we have relationships—coworkers, family members, neighbors, and friends. Christ does not give us the liberty to hold grudges and harbor unforgiveness against people just because they are unbelievers. Rather, he challenges us to consider them with the same heart of compassion and forgiveness we would our Christian family.

Christ felt so strongly about this point that he linked it to the promise of unanswered prayer: "And *when you stand praying...*forgive." If we want the promise of verse 24, we

What Do I

Do with the

Pain?

❖

35

must live out the charge of verse 25. If we pray for healing in our lives or in others' but retain bitterness and unforgiveness toward another person, God has the right to withhold answering our prayers. Unforgiveness, simply put, disqualifies our prayers.

It is interesting to note that in 1 Peter 3:7, the Bible tells husbands that their prayers will not be answered if they do not have a proper relationship with their wives. Husbands are told to understand their wives, to honor them, and to share the grace of life with them so that nothing will hinder their prayers. Husbands can struggle with problems in business, their personal lives, their finances, or even problems with their children because they have failed to meet their wives' needs. God remains silent because they have not honored their wives.

In most cases where tension exists in a marriage, it is because one or both partners have failed to forgive the other. The greatest dishonor we can show each other is to be unforgiving.

Unforgiveness in our hearts can be the greatest hindrance to effective praying. We must be careful to deal with the issues of forgiveness toward others before we can expect God to heal us.

REFUSAL TO FORGIVE OTHERS CAN KEEP GOD FROM FORGIVING US

"If you do not forgive, neither will your Father…forgive your sins" (Mark 11:26). We read a similar statement in

Matthew 6:15: "But if you do not forgive men their sins, your Father will not forgive your sins."

Christ tells us that if we do not exercise forgiveness toward others, our own sins will not be forgiven us. Although God has a great flood tide of forgiveness for us, he is bound to restrain it until we ourselves forgive those who have wronged us. He is willing to forgive all our sins, mistakes, and blunders by the power of the blood of Christ, but we will never know that forgiveness until we are willing to forgive others.

$\mathscr{C}$HRIST— OUR GREAT EXAMPLE

Christ is our prime example for forgiving others. It was a horrible, glorious day in history. So much had happened in the previous twenty-four hours that we cannot begin to comprehend. Less than a day before, Christ had been spending time with his disciples in prayer at the Garden of Gethsemane. Gethsemane was the place where olives were pressed into oil with the millstones. The crushing weight of the huge stones would squeeze the very juices out of the fruit until it was a lifeless pulp. Christ felt a similar weight upon himself that night, knowing that he would offer up his life for humankind.

Imagine the dusky sky illuminating the city below as he prayed in the garden. Visualize a line of torches moving up the mountain like glowing ants. Imagine the feelings Christ must have experienced, knowing that those lights were carried by soldiers coming to arrest him. Imagine the thoughts that ran through his mind since he knew that Judas, one of the twelve, was leading the way.

Judas was the one whom most of his contemporaries viewed as successful. He was a go-getter and a manager of money. He was known for his business ability and had been given great responsibility. Even those close to him trusted him and gave him charge of the books. But his strength was also his weakness. He was trusted by the other disciples to the very end, to the extent that they thought he left the Passover meal to make payments for the food or to the charities. That departure was instead his dismissal by Christ to do what he was to do, namely to betray Christ. Scripture tells us that he was a thief and stole from the money bags (see John 12:6). His greed for money led him to the priests that night. Have you ever had anyone betray you?

Another man who deeply hurt Jesus was Simon Peter. Peter was one of the inner circle of the disciples. Whenever Jesus drew his intimate circle to him, Peter was there. Peter was a man of common interests and upbringing. He was also a tradesman, a fisherman. Unlike Judas, his interests were spending time with a select few, building relationships, and sharing dreams. His love for Jesus was incomparable. Many events prove this: walking on the water to meet Jesus, declaring his desire to build him a temple, proclaiming undying devotion, and even jeopardizing his own life by attacking one of the Roman guards who came to take Christ away. Peter's devotion was so strong that he and John were the only disciples (as far as Scripture says) who followed Christ and his captors to the house of the high priest.

But we also read that on the night of Jesus' trial, when observers asked Peter if he was one of Jesus' followers, he quickly denied his association three separate times (see Luke 22). Upon the third denial, Christ looked at Peter with knowing eyes and all could hear the cock crow, according to prophecy. This same man who declared undying allegiance to Christ had denied him.

As Christ was hanging on the cross just a few hours later, he said some of the most profound and convicting words of exhortation. He had been beaten, he was bleeding, and he had a crown of thorns on his head. He had been mocked and spit upon. His closest friends had deserted him, betrayed him, and hid from him. With these events in the forefront of his mind, yet having a heart of compassion, he cried out, "Father, forgive them, for they do not know what they are doing" (Luke 23:34).

If Jesus could forgive us, how can we not forgive those who have wronged us? The real heart of the matter of forgiveness is realizing that God is greater than all our hurts. He can deal with those who wrong us if we are willing to forgive them. Who has hurt you? Your wife, your husband, your parents, an ex-wife, an ex-husband, a former business partner, your boss, or your friend? Whoever they may be, God can enable you to fully and completely forgive them.

In Matthew 18:21, Peter asked Jesus about the law of forgiveness: "Lord, how many times shall I forgive my brother when he sins against me?" Then Peter, thinking he was being generous, doubled the number that the Pharisees had prescribed and added one: "Seven times?" Peter's generosity paled in comparison to Christ's response of "seventy-seven times." This was not intended to be a specific number but an exaggerated hyperbole meaning infinite and without end.

Why? Because it's the character of God to have complete, total, everlasting forgiveness. We must be willing to admit that we have feelings against someone and confess them before God. If we do that, God is willing and waiting to forgive us. Only we and our attitudes of unforgiveness stand in the way of God's healing in our lives. Christ's words ring just as true today as they did two thousand years ago when he said, "If you forgive men when they sin against you, your heavenly Father will also forgive you" (Matthew 6:14).

BLESSINGS UNLEASHED!

When we forgive, we unleash the dynamic and powerful blessings of God upon our lives. First Peter 3:8–9 states it clearly: "Finally, all of you, live in harmony with one another; be sympathetic, love as brothers, be compassionate and humble. Do not repay evil with evil or insult with insult, but with blessing, because to this you were called so that you may inherit a blessing." This verse shows us that if we live in a spirit of compassion and love, caring for one another, not bearing a grudge, but forgiving one another, we will inherit untold blessings from God. These blessings include mercy shown to us by God and others, a restoration of joy in our lives, and a spirit of love and peace toward others.

In 2 Corinthians 2:6–11, Paul urges the church at Corinth to forgive a brother who had sinned, because refusal to forgive is one of the most effective tools Satan uses in his attempts to destroy us. Paul told them to forgive "in order that Satan might not outwit us. For we are not unaware of his schemes" (v. 11). In his book *The Freedom and Power of Forgiveness*, John MacArthur says,

> Satan's whole agenda is undermined by forgiveness. If forgiveness deflects pride, shows mercy, restores joy, affirms mercy, proves obedience, and revitalizes fellowship, imagine how Satan must hate it! Therefore, forgiveness is an essential part of undoing Satan's schemes.... Forgiveness then is the soil in which numerous spiritual fruits and divine blessings are cultivated. Tending and nurturing the soil of forgiveness is one of the surest ways to develop spiritual health and maturity.[3]

Simply put, in our search for healing, forgiveness is a vital key. Without it, we will do no more than what we can do in our own flesh. But with forgiveness playing out its divine role in our minds and hearts, God's power will be released in our behalf and the healing touch of Jesus will have already begun!

CHAPTER

Are you ready to begin the process of forgiving those who have wronged you? Are you convinced that forgiving others is an essential step in the process of finding healing for ourselves? If so, you may have some questions about what it really means to forgive. We'll look at it from two angles: what forgiveness is and what it's not.

❖

42

---

*W*HAT FORGIVENESS IS NOT

❖ *It is not forgetting with no recall.*
Many offenses, because of their damaging nature, would be impossible to completely forget.

❖ *It is not condoning or approving an act that someone committed against us.*
Right is still right, and wrong is still wrong.

❖ *It is not ignoring the consequences of the offense.*
The fact remains that every action of life has consequences.

❖ *It is not treating the offense as if it never happened.*
We need to remember how offenses take place so that we might avoid them in the future.

❖ *It is not demanding that a close relationship be forced between the offended and the offender.*
Some relationships are healthier for both parties when encounters are less frequent.

What Forgiveness Really Is

WHAT FORGIVENESS REALLY IS

* *It is understanding the nature of the offense.*
  You cannot forgive another without first understanding how you were offended and why you feel
  as you do.

* *It is the acknowledgment of the depth of your hurt.*
  It is foolish to have a flippant, carefree attitude on
  the surface when there is a real and deep hurt
  within. This will only prolong and deepen the pain.

* *It is agreeing with God concerning the need to forgive.*
  We have come to a heartfelt conviction that forgiveness is the right way to handle our situation.

* *It is making a conscious decision to forgive and then
  taking action upon that decision.*
  To decide to forgive is the first step. Finding God's
  direction about what you need "to do" and "doing
  it" is essential.

* *It is asking God to take the hurt and anger from your
  heart.*
  After all is done, the healing process must be com-
  pleted by the power of the Holy Spirit in your life.

$\mathcal{A}$s he went along, he saw a man blind from birth. His disciples asked him, "Rabbi, who sinned, this man or his parents, that he was born blind?"

"Neither this man nor his parents sinned," said Jesus, "but this happened so that the work of God might be displayed in his life. As long as it is day, we must do the work of him who sent me. Night is coming, when no one can work."

—*John 9:1–4*

Chapter Four

WHY DO CHRISTIANS SUFFER?

The Hidden Blessings of Pain

Pain and *suffering*: Without a doubt these are two of the hardest subjects to deal with. We consistently ask, "Why do Christians suffer? Christians are supposed to have joy and peace and prosperity; so why do we suffer?" That question is not so easily answered—especially when a Christian is struggling with personal or family illness.

Part of the problem is that many misunderstand what it means to be a Christian. Being a Christian does not mean we will never have pain or sickness or suffering. But it does mean that we will have enough strength and peace and joy to make it through. In 2 Corinthians, Paul identifies why we, as Christians, sometimes have to suffer. In fact, even Christ speaks of the fact that we will be persecuted and endure suffering for his sake. I believe that this sometimes includes personal illness, no matter how close we are to God. Why? So that God can receive glory when our healing comes.

One day, while Jesus and his disciples were walking through Jerusalem, they saw a man who had been born blind (see John 9). The disciples asked Jesus whose sin had caused this man's condition—his own or his parents'. They assumed that suffering is always the result of someone's personal sin. Christ responded that the man's condition was not caused by sin at all; "but this happened so that the work of God might be displayed in his life" (v. 3). Jesus then used this opportunity not only to perform a miracle but to bring God glory.

Christ proceeded to spit on the ground and make a clay pack that he put on the man's eyes. Then he sent the man to the pool of Siloam to wash, and the man's eyes were healed. Those who had known the blind man all his life were incredulous! "Isn't this the same man who used to sit and beg?" (v. 8). When they took him to be examined by the Pharisees, they wouldn't believe he'd been born blind until they interrogated his parents. As much as they didn't want to believe that this man had been healed, they could not argue the fact that he had gained his sight.

How did God receive glory in this? First, the event increased the disciples' faith. During these first months of Christ's ministry, his disciples were still fluctuating in their faith that he was the Messiah. Each miracle brought them closer to a deeper knowledge that Jesus was the Christ. So in our lives, each event should bring us to a deeper knowledge of Christ.

Second, the man declared his faith in Jesus when Jesus found him in the temple court. What better reward for our sufferings than to see a person, possibly a loved one, come to salvation through the testimony of our experiences?

Throughout all of the New Testament, we see men and women who suffered for Christ's sake. That suffering came in many forms: illness, injury, persecution, and misunderstanding. The apostle Paul is a prime example.

Both the Romans and the Jews had issues with Paul and his work. The Jews were upset that he turned from being a zealous persecutor of Christians to become a devoted follower of the man Jesus. They were unable to forgive him for betraying them and preaching that Jesus was the Christ. The Romans persecuted Paul because his teachings angered the Jews, which made their job of keeping the peace more difficult. While Paul had opposed the Christian sect, he had appeased the Jewish leaders. But when he joined the Christian forces, the Jewish leaders became more antagonistic and angry, which led to increased chaos. The Roman government blamed Paul for the riots and unrest that surrounded him (see Acts 19–23). In fact, men from both arenas sought to capture Paul and execute him.

Not only was Paul attacked by nonbelievers, but his character and authority as a minister of the gospel were questioned by Christians in Corinth. Have you ever had a friend betray you? The pain and the hurt are sometimes greater than physical suffering. And yet, this is what Paul had to deal with. Some in the church at Corinth did not appreciate Paul's preaching. Their immoral lifestyles were challenged by Paul's instruction. Perhaps they thought that by turning the tables, their own lifestyles could be left uninvestigated, and they could continue living the way they chose. They attacked Paul's apostleship, and they attacked the authority of his calling. Their accusations caused Paul suffering and grief, yet he began his second epistle to them by gently encouraging them with teachings of God's comfort and instructing them about suffering.

Why did God allow Paul to suffer? Why does he allow us to suffer? In 2 Corinthians 1, Paul gives us five specific reasons that Christians suffer and how that suffering brings glory to God.

#1: THROUGH OUR SUFFERING, WE CAN COMFORT OTHERS

Paul says that when we suffer and receive God's comfort, we are then able to comfort others who suffer: "The Father of compassion and the God of all comfort…comforts us in all our troubles, so that we can comfort those in any trouble with the comfort we ourselves have received from God" (2 Corinthians 1:3–4). In these two short verses, the word *comfort* is used four times. Note also that Paul does not ascribe comfort to us but tells us that the source of that comfort is God himself. When we suffer, it gives us the ability to comfort each other and direct each other to the source of our comfort.

As our Comforter, God remains by our sides to love us, help us, strengthen us, and encourage us. But his comforting is not for us alone, for we are encouraged to help others in their sufferings. It is only by his working in our lives and by the power of God as the Comforter who dwells in us that we are able to act as comforters to others in the hurt and pain of their lives.

In John 14:15–18, we discover that the source of our comfort is the "Comforter," the Holy Spirit. However, some people try to rely on their own power when comforting others—using their own words or actions—rather than relying on the divine Comforter. These self-appointed comforters tend to do more harm than good. Have you ever had someone try to comfort you, but their efforts left you feeling the same or worse? Often this happens because we don't rely on the Spirit to speak through us, but we say what we want to say. Those times become more of a discouragement than a time of healing.

Paul understood the persecution that some of the church members were going through because he had been through it too. Only when we walk in the valleys do we know what the valley is like. And when others are going through that valley, we can understand their pain and bring the Comforter alongside to bless and soothe their troubled hearts.

#2: OUR SUFFERING CAN MANIFEST CHRIST'S SUFFICIENCY

To the degree of our need, Christ demonstrates his sufficiency. He matches every heartache, heartbreak, despair, and discouragement with love, comfort, peace, and strength. The Living Bible says "You can be sure that the more we undergo sufferings for Christ, the more he will shower us with his comfort and encouragement" (2 Corinthians 1:5). How can we know the strength of Christ in our lives if we do not experience situations that require his power? If life were only good and happy and positive, we would not recognize our need for Christ. It is when the bad and the ugly occur that we call on him to comfort us and provide strength.

Often in Scripture, God encourages us to stop relying on ourselves and to turn to him to provide for our needs. We are not sufficient within ourselves to handle life's problems. It is when life gets tough that Christ steps in and becomes our sufficiency. The Book of Hebrews tells us that Christ is able to sympathize with us in our time of need because he has been through the same situations we face. And because Jesus understands, the Hebrew writer says we are able to approach Jesus boldly. And when we approach him, we find mercy and grace to help us (see 4:15–16).

If life were a "piece of cake," how would we ever discover the power and mercy of God? We wouldn't! We can never know the strength of something or someone until it is tested. God's sufficiency can be put to the test in our everyday lives. You will find him strong on behalf of his children.

#3: OUR SUFFERING CAUSES US TO RELY ON GOD ALONE

When we suffer, according to Paul, we learn to trust in God alone (see 2 Corinthians 8–10). Paul experienced a situation in Asia that caused him to have great despair. History does not give all of the details, but it is likely that he's alluding to a riot in the city of Ephesus (see Acts 19:23–41), when the city rose up against him and tried to kill him. Paul was so disturbed by this that he thought "the sentence of death" was upon his life. Down, dejected, and discouraged beyond compare, Paul was challenged to rely not on himself but on God alone.

Have you ever been in a situation when you have felt it would be easier to die than to make it through? So often in the difficult times in our lives, we fall away from God, growing more and more distant from him when all he wants is for us to draw closer to him. He wants this so that we can learn to rely on him alone. Even the great apostle Paul could not make it alone. Why do we think we can?

Look at the Old Testament and King David for another example of utter trust in God. Over and over in the psalms, we read of David's despair and hopelessness. During his flight from Saul, he was constantly afraid for his life. David knew what betrayal and abandonment meant. Yet his psalms reflect not only on his despair and fear but on his trust in God's provision and strength and on the peace he finds in God's power.

As a Jew, Paul surely studied David's great example of

dependence on God. He learned from this king that God will deliver his children, and he imparted that comforting knowledge to the Corinthian church: "He has delivered us from such a deadly peril, and he will deliver us. On him we have set our hope that he will continue to deliver us" (2 Corinthians 1:10). Paul trusted not only in God's past deliverance; he also believed that God is presently working to deliver us. Beyond that, Paul believed that in the future, God will give us the blessed peace of complete deliverance from suffering. Paul made sure to mention past, present, and future to remind us that Jesus is forever by our sides.

#4: $\mathcal{S}$UFFERING ENCOURAGES PRAYER AND THANKSGIVING

Nothing drives us to our knees like trouble, and nothing makes us more thankful than when we are delivered from that trouble. Thankfulness comes from the hearts of people who have received deliverance from trials in their lives. Christ tells a parable of a man who received forgiveness of a great debt and another man who received forgiveness of a small debt. He then asked the disciples which one was more thankful. They responded that the one who was forgiven more was the more thankful. Christ confirmed their answer, saying that the more a person is forgiven, the more thankful and loving that person is (see Luke 7:41–47).

But thankfulness alone is not enough. We also need to be compassionate and caring toward one another. We remember the story of the Pharisee who cried out in the temple that he was thankful that he was not like the sinner. But God was displeased with the Pharisee's prayer because he had no compassion on others. We must also learn to pray for one another. Second Corinthians 1:10–11 says, "He will continue to deliver us, as you help us by your prayers. Then many will give thanks on our behalf for the gracious favor granted us in answer to the prayers of many." As we endure suffering, we are to intercede for others on their behalf, having gone through similar circumstances. The truth of the matter is that intercessory prayer works. When you pray for another in their hardship or need, God hears and answers that prayer. Paul tells the Corinthians that their prayers made a difference. That is the reason they should be thankful.

In your own life, you have probably known people who have interceded and prayed for you: a parent, a friend, a pastor. When we seek God's face on others' behalf, God is moved with compassion and responds. He loves it when his children gain his heart for the world and look on it with compassion. That is why intercessory prayer works.

In my office I have a wonderful three-pound stone from the Garden of Gethsemane. I received it several years ago from one of the offices of the government of Israel. It is a piece of a larger rock believed to be the rock upon which Jesus prayed that night before his crucifixion so long ago. I often look at that stone and think of the story it could tell if the stones could only cry out!

Two of the most powerful prayers of intercession in

Scripture are from Christ himself. The first was in that garden called Gethsemane. Jesus was about to face his tough-
est decision—he was about to lay down his life for the sins
of mankind. He was aware that at that very time, Judas was
informing the Sanhedrin of his whereabouts. In his divine
knowledge, he knew that death was coming. He spent his
first words of prayer begging God for another way. Knowing
that there was no other way, he yielded himself in obedience and turned his focus on those he would leave behind
(see John 17:6–26). He prayed first for his disciples: He
prayed for their protection, their empowerment, their
strength, and that their walk be strong. He then prayed for
us—those who would believe the word of the disciples.
Jesus Christ interceded on our behalf and prayed to the
Father that we would be one with him and follow after him
and glorify the Father.

The second intercessory prayer is a very short one.
While Christ was suffering the crucifixion of the cross, he
cried out to the Father, "Father, forgive them, for they do
not know what they are doing" (Luke 23:34). Christ, in the
midst of his greatest suffering, used that suffering as an
opportunity to intercede on our behalf.

#5: $\mathscr{S}$UFFERING TEACHES US TO CLAIM THE PROMISES OF GOD

When God makes a promise, you can count on it. It is
always right. As humans, we often make promises we can-

not or do not keep. Even Paul made a promise to the people of Corinth that he couldn't keep. He had promised to come to visit them, but because of circumstances and problems, he was prevented from coming as planned. Some in the church attacked him, calling him a liar and untrustworthy. They even questioned his apostleship. Paul replies in 2 Corinthians 1:15–18 that his intentions were genuine but that he was unable to fulfill his promise. He then contrasts his human failing with the faithfulness of God. He explains that we can depend on God for every circumstance. God does not break his promises but fulfills every one of them. People make promises and often cannot keep them, but God always fulfills his promises. The death and resurrection power of Christ assures it. Whatever promise God has made to you, not only does he have the power to keep it, but rest assured, he will!

Quite often we suffer without understanding what God is doing in our lives. As a result, the suffering seems more intense and unbearable. But if we gain the right perspective and begin to see how God is using the suffering in our own lives to conform us to his image, we will understand and trust God's hand in our lives.

While God is not the source of our suffering, he uses what Satan throws against us to our benefit. God turns Satan's flaming arrows into showers of blessing. We see many great men of faith throughout the Old Testament who suffered, including Moses, David, Jeremiah, and especially

❖

Joseph. Our desire is that one day we would be able to pro-claim, as Joseph did, that "God intended it for good" (Genesis 50:20).

Knowing that suffering can be for his glory is all well and good, but what about when we don't hear or see God at all? Next, we will examine our response when it seems God is silent to our cries. How should we respond when we come face to face with "the God who isn't there"?

❖

*W*ithout faith it is impossible to please God, because anyone who comes to him must believe that he exists and that he rewards those who earnestly seek him.

—Hebrews 11:6

Chapter Five

IS GOD REALLY THERE?

Overcoming Barriers to Prayer

Several days ago, I was visited by a dear lady who was at the end of her rope. She felt exasperated and alone. She told me that she felt God had abandoned her. "No matter how hard I pray," she said, "God just doesn't answer me."

"What kind of answer are you wanting?" I asked.

"One that says yes to my needs, of course," she replied.

"Well, my understanding is that God doesn't always say yes," I suggested. "He can see much farther down the road than we can, so he sometimes tells us no for our own good."

"That's not what I want to hear," she stated.

"I know it may not be what you *want* to hear," I answered, "but it just may be just what you *need* to hear."

$\mathcal{D}$OES GOD
HEAR MY PRAYERS?

CHAPTER

5

❖

60

When our prayers aren't answered exactly as we expect them to be, sometimes we doubt that God hears us at all; we wonder whether he really cares. The problem is not that God doesn't hear or care; it may be that we do not understand how God answers prayers. When we don't get the answer we expect, there's often a very good reason.

SOMETIMES GOD SAYS NO

James 4:3 says, "When you ask, you do not receive, because you ask with wrong motives." When your motive for asking is not right, God will not grant your requests. He has not deserted you. He is still there—but he is denying your request for your own good. We cannot expect God to contradict his own wisdom and give us something that is not good for us simply because we demand it.

God is omniscient, or all-knowing. He knows all about us. Our past and our future are ever present before the mind of God. Because our God is loving and knows everything that ever will be, he sometimes says no when saying yes would ultimately hurt us.

We find a classic example of this kind of answer in 1 Kings 19:1–4. As God's spokesman, Elijah the prophet called down the fire of God on the altar on Mount Carmel. He had slain the prophets of Baal and called down judgment on the royal family of Israel. But when wicked Queen Jezebel determined to kill him, he fled for his life. He escaped into the wilderness and took shelter under a broom tree. There, in total exhaustion, he begged God to take his life. But God said no.

Elijah didn't really want to die. If that had been the case, he could just as well have stayed in town. Jezebel would have been glad to accommodate him. Elijah was simply looking for an easy way out of his troubles. He wanted to pull the ejection cord and catapult out the escape hatch of life. But God said no for his own good.

We are all often guilty of the same kind of selfish requests. We want God to bail us out of our troubles, when he wants to use those troubles to mold and shape our lives. In reality, he is often protecting us from our own selfishness and greed. Sometimes when he says no, he is being there when we need him most by saying no for our own good.

Sometimes God Says Wait

In Ecclesiastes 3:1, we read: "There is a time for everything, and a season for every activity under heaven." Timing is crucial to almost everything is life. This is especially true in athletics. It does not matter how much physical ability an athlete has, he will not be a winner if he cannot achieve the proper timing. There have been many baseball players, for example, who had the strength to hit home runs but could not time the swing of their bat to meet the ball properly, and they failed to make it in baseball.

This principle is often true in our daily lives. Even when

we desire something within the will of God for ourselves, we must be willing to wait for his timing to bring it to pass. God never promised to answer our prayers on our timetable. There is not one guarantee in Scripture that he will always give us what we want when we want it.

We live in an instantaneous age. We want everything right now. That is why we have fast food and instant coffee. Our generation knows little or nothing about delayed gratification. There was a time when people had to wait a long time to be able to afford something they wanted. Now, we just lay down a credit card and take it home.

When we turn to God in prayer, we expect the same results. Unfortunately, that is not how God works. He moves on his schedule, not ours. He is our Father, and we are his children. You can place your complete trust in the One who made time. He knows us best and always operates on schedule.

Sometimes God Provides a New Direction

Often, the paths we take in life lead us down roads that bring us harm. But if we are open to his leading, God lovingly, yet firmly, directs us back on the proper path. Choosing the right path isn't always a priority when things are going well, but when the bottom falls out, God can often get our attention in a hurry. In times of trouble, we are usually quick to reexamine ourselves in the light of his direction.

Jonah was a prophet of God who got off course. God

commanded him to go east to Nineveh, the Assyrian capital, to preach to the enemies of Israel. Instead, he fled in the opposite direction. He went down to the Mediterranean seacoast town of Joppa and took a ship headed west to Tarshish. Exhausted, he fell sound asleep in the ship, only to be awakened by a violent storm. The Bible declares that God sent the storm deliberately because Jonah was running away from God's will. In desperation, and perhaps out of guilt, Jonah told the mariners to throw him overboard to appease the wrath of God.

❖

There are lots of people just like Jonah. They are moving in a direction opposite to God's will for their lives, and he sends a storm to get their attention. It's at this point that each person must choose how to react. Some, instead of repenting and changing direction, want to end it all by a self-destructive act, or they rebel and continue on their path. These are never the right responses. God is greater than our problems, and he always provides a way out (see 1 Corinthians 10:13). On the other hand, those who are willing to heed his instruction will find that he has a plan and a purpose for every one of his children—even if that purpose is sometimes revealed in the belly of a whale.

For you see, at the moment of Jonah's greatest desperation, "the LORD provided a great fish" (Jonah 1:17). Jonah wasn't swallowed by accident, but by divine purpose. Aside from another ship, this was the only way God could get Jonah to Nineveh to carry out his plan. What was the first thing Jonah did in the belly of the whale? The Bible says,

"Jonah prayed" (2:1). He didn't pray when he decided to run away. He didn't pray when he first entered the ship and fell asleep. He prayed when he was face to face with a desperate situation. In the depth of his troubles, he called out to God, and God redirected his course.

Sometimes, like Jonah, we know what God wants us to do, but we are unwilling to do it. In our rebellion, we devise our own clever plans that exclude God from our lives. When we think we have escaped his notice, he sends a storm into our lives to get our attention. Why does he do this? Simply because he knows that these troubles will cause us to reexamine our priorities and put our lives back on course with his will and purpose.

*B*ARRIERS TO ANSWERED PRAYER

But often, our problem is not about the *kind* of answer God gives us; sometimes it's that we feel as if he's not answering us at all. Do you ever feel as if your prayers are bouncing off the ceiling? Does it ever seem that God answers the prayers of others, but not yours? Do you feel that you're praying to a God who isn't there? This next section will help you discover some of the barriers we unwittingly set up between ourselves and God. These barriers leave us feeling cut off and distant from God; we feel abandoned and wonder if he is even real. Tearing down these self-imposed barriers will bring you into the sweet relationship with God that you crave.

The first reason we don't get the answers we want is that we fail to make our requests known. Sounds strange, doesn't it? How could anyone expect to have prayers answered when they are never prayed? Yet many times we do just that. The excuses range from, "God knows what I need, so why do I need to ask for it?" to "My request is too small to bother God with" or "My problem is too big to bother God with." But these assumptions are based on strange and unscriptural views on prayer. The Book of James tells us that we do not receive because we do not ask (see 4:2). And Philippians 4:6 says that we should make our requests known to God.

Sometimes we equate prayer with wishful thinking. We use our imagination like children: We sit and imagine our needs in our minds and visualize how we think God will answer those needs. We expect our imaginary scenarios to play out in real life—as if God were a genie in a bottle. Unfortunately, our fantasies do not pan out. Then we get disappointed with God because we have misunderstood how he works in our lives.

"LAST-RESORT" PRAYERS

Often times, we use prayer as our spiritual last resort. We work and try and sweat out our own solutions to life until we get everything tangled up. Then we cry out to God to come and rescue us and fix what we have messed up. Have you ever said, "I guess I should pray about this, since nothing else has worked"? I sure have. It seems that we use God as our last resort instead of our first. This is not the way God intended it to be. In fact, we can mess things up so much that God has to come and search us out. Look at Adam in the Garden. Adam had a great relationship with God. Everything was perfect, and he walked daily beside God in the Garden and asked questions to his heart's delight. But after that sinful event of eating the fruit of the tree of knowledge, Adam realized he had messed things up. But instead of approaching God with his need for forgiveness and then admitting his failure, he tried to fix the problem himself. So he searched the Garden for leaves as a covering, not only of his physical vulnerability but of his now sinful nature. When God came searching him out, Adam attempted to hide. We come by this naturally, following in our earthly father's footsteps. We try to cover up our mistakes or fix them on our own instead of running straight to God for help—as a *first* resort.

But Christ gives us a solution to that problem. Matthew 21:22 says, "If you believe, you will receive whatever you ask for in prayer."

Our Own Will

Another barrier we place between ourselves and God is our own stubborn will. During Jesus' last few hours on earth, he begged the Father for another way; but he concluded his prayer in submission to God: "Yet not as I will, but as you will" (Matthew 26:39). So often in our prayers, we pray more "my will be done" than God's will be done.

In the darkest days during the war between the states,

General Robert E. Lee went into a church to pray. As he exited, he was asked if he was praying for victory. His response was, "No, I'm praying for God's will to be done." No matter how much faith we think we have, and no matter how often and persistent we are in our prayers, if we are not praying for God's will, then we won't receive the response we expect from God. First John 5:14 says that we have confidence "that if we ask anything according to his will, he hears us."

But how do we know the will of God? Knowing the will of God is not a hard task; abiding in God is. Christ specifically instructs us, "If you abide in me, and my words abide in you, ask whatever you will, and it shall be done for you" (John 15:7 RSV). Christ never had a problem with understanding the will of God because he abode in the Father. And we abide in him when we read his Word. God gave us specific instructions on what his will for our lives is. These instructions are called the Bible. The Bible is our instruction manual for life. When we meditate on the Word, God will illuminate our minds, and we will not struggle with the issues of what God's will is in these circumstances.

WRONG MOTIVES

James 4:3 tells us that sometimes we do not receive because we ask with wrong motives, that we may spend what we get on our own pleasures. We even see in Matthew 20:21 that when the mother of James and John asked that her sons be seated on the left and right of the throne of Christ, Jesus rebuked her, saying, "You don't know what you are asking"

(v. 22). He explained that such a request was not even his to grant but would be determined by God the Father. In similar ways, we ask of God things we should not. Humanly speaking, we cannot see the whole picture of God's design for our lives. Because of this limitation, we can ask for things that are not for our good or are not in God's time frame.

Nowhere in Scripture does God promise to always give us all that we want. How many times would your life have been ruined if God had given what you had selfishly prayed for? Remember, God is too wise to help us destroy ourselves with selfish desires.

When we are self-centered and pray with selfish motives and desires, God often says no for our own good because he loves us and wants to give us what is best.

Some people act like the spoiled little boy who lived down the street from me when I was a child. When he did not get his way with his parents, he would hold his breath, turn several shades of red, and fall to the floor, flailing his hands and feet. His parents would immediately cave in to his desires. But one afternoon when he was visiting our home, he learned an important lesson from my mother. Something happened that afternoon, and he did not get his way. So, true to form, he held his breath and fell to the floor, red-faced. My mother's response was to fold her arms and chuckle at him. This continued for a few minutes until he sat up, gasping for breath, and then ran home. Mother knew that it is impossible to hold your breath until you die! His tantrums didn't impress her at all.

Likewise, our spiritual tantrums do not impress God. How do we throw a spiritual tantrum? Often we do so in the form of coercion or threats toward God. "God, you didn't answer my prayer so you must not be up there." "God, if you don't give me this or that, I'll stop going to church." "God, if I don't get what I asked for, I'm going to stop tithing." We must realize that we cannot coerce or shame God into acting how we want him to act. Some folks just need to grow up and realize that wrong motives that lead to wrong actions get no response from God.

BITTERNESS

Bitterness toward others can actually inhibit our prayers. Speaking to husbands about their relationships with their wives, 1 Peter 3:7 says, "Husbands,…be considerate as you live with your wives, and treat them with respect as the weaker partner and as heirs with you of the gracious gift of life, so that nothing will hinder your prayers." Did you catch the last phrase, "so that nothing will hinder your prayers"? How we deal with one another not only separates us from those here on earth, it can create a barrier between us and God. How we treat our families—husbands, wives, children, parents—is important to God.

Hebrews 12:15 exhorts us further: "See to it that no one misses the grace of God and that no bitter root grows up to cause trouble and defile many." The word *defile* means to stain. Many times our hearts are stained because of bitterness we harbor toward those who have wronged us. Several times in Scripture, Christ commands us to make things right with others. In Matthew 5:23–24, Jesus tells us that before we offer anything to him, we must make things right with our brother. In Colossians 3:13, Paul instructs us that we have a responsibility to forgive others because Christ forgave us. Bitterness can be a great hindrance to our prayers and a barrier to God's throne.

REFUSING GODLY COUNSEL

God places godly people in our lives. Many times they speak to the situations in our lives and give us his counsel. When we refuse their counsel, it can hinder our prayer life. In the Book of Zechariah, we find an unusual story of what happened when counsel was not heeded. Zechariah was a prophet of God who was sent to the nation of Israel to give them a warning. He proclaimed the message of God to them, but they "refused to pay attention; stubbornly they turned their backs and stopped up their ears. They made their hearts as hard as flint and would not listen to the law or to the words that the LORD Almighty had sent by his Spirit through the earlier prophets" (7:11–12). Zechariah went on to say: " 'When I called, they did not listen; so when they called, I would not listen,' says the LORD Almighty" (v. 13). They had turned a deaf ear to the message and messenger of God, and God's response was to turn a deaf ear to them. In the Book of Luke, we see a similar response from Jesus: When he sent the apostles out to preach, he told them that if someone did not receive them, they should shake the dust off their feet as a testimony against them. When God speaks to us through others, we must take care to listen and heed his words.

An Unclean Heart

Finally, we inhibit our prayers to God when we attempt to come before him with unclean hearts. David says in Psalm 66:18, "If I had cherished sin in my heart, the Lord would not have listened." Over and over in the Bible, we see that unconfessed sin cuts us off from the Holy God. In Psalm 66, David is speaking about *cherished* sin, which means sin that we hold on to and are not willing to give up. But God calls us to repent of all sin. To repent simply means to turn away from, to go the opposite direction of, to flee from. Now, I understand that some sins are a real struggle, but if we harbor any sin and are not willing to give it up for God, Scripture tells us that it becomes a barrier to our relationship with him.

Years ago, the king of England visited a dilapidated, run-down cobbler's shop in southern England. As he walked in, he noticed the filth of the unkempt walls and floor and the clutter behind the counter. When the owner recognized the king, he bowed down before him and apologized for the mess. The king told him he would return the next day and if the cobbler would clean up the building, he would bless it. The next day, the king returned to find a building swept clean and sparkling, so he hung a sign over the shop's doorway that read, "APPROVED BY THE KING." From then on, the cobbler never lacked for business, for he was approved by the king.

Likewise, God desires for us to have a clean life. As the King of kings visits our hearts, does he find it clean of sin or filled with the dirt of unconfessed sin? He desires to give us his seal of approval. He asks that we would clean our hearts out so that he can commune with us and that nothing would block our prayers with him. If we repent from our sins and follow the steps that have been provided for us in Scripture, heaven will stand at attention when we pray. And God will answer our prayers.

𝒫RAYER STRATEGY

Now that we've identified some of the barriers to prayer, let's learn how to break through those barriers and enter God's throne room. And who better to learn from than Jesus himself? "One day, while Jesus was praying…his disciples said to him, 'Lord, teach us to pray.'"

Now, the disciples had grown up in Jewish society and would have known how to pray, but they saw something different in Jesus' prayers. His prayers had power, and when he prayed, God worked. They were not simply asking Jesus to teach them a form of prayer, they were asking how to be effective in prayer. Christ taught them the techniques of effective prayer. Matthew 6 gives us that model prayer in which he shared the strategy for approaching God's throne.

The first thing we should always do in our prayers is

acknowledge God for who he is. Christ did this in two ways. First, he acknowledged that God is a loving and caring Father. But he did not forget that God is also a righteous and holy God. We must be sure to balance these two aspects in our view of God. If we view God only as a loving Father, we set ourselves up for disappointment when he does not do what we ask. This one-sided view makes God out to be a spiritual Santa Claus who is only there to give us what we ask. But when we balance his loving-kindness with his righteousness and holiness, we realize that God gives us what is best because he knows best what we need.

❖

The next ingredient in Christ's prayer model was acknowledgment of God's sovereignty. "Your kingdom come, your will be done." This proclamation acknowledges that we submit to his will regardless of our own. We need to give God the place that is due him in the grand scheme of things. By recognizing his will as the greatest will, we allow him to work his will in us, and we lay down our own will in the process.

Christ then asks for God's provision. Christ does not ask for extraordinary events but for daily bread. This kind of prayer is a statement of faith that God will provide for our needs on a daily basis.

Next, Christ prayed that the relationship of forgiveness that we have with the Father be lived out in our earthly relationships. This includes forgiving, accepting, and being content with our family, friends, and business.

Christ also taught us to pray for protection from the evil

in the world and to ask God to show us a clear way of escape in times of temptation.

Jesus concluded the model prayer by acknowledging who God is and his ability and power to accomplish these things in our lives.

If we want to have a successful prayer life and be assured that God hears our prayers, we must persistently apply the principles Christ taught us in his model prayer. God did not leave the matter of prayer a mystery for us to struggle with and guess at; rather, he provided clear directions on how we communicate with him. We should never feel inadequate to approach God with our needs. We were designed to communicate with him and to trust him to provide for us.

❖

The truth of the matter is that the God who isn't there—is there! He is waiting and willing to bring us healing, restoration, and blessings, but we must do our part. So with our motives pure, our wills in submission to his, the roots of bitterness dug up and cast away, our hearts swept clean by confession, and our ears open to his counsel, we are able to come boldly into his presence, confident that whatever we ask according to his will is ours. That is God's promise. That is our sure hope.

$\mathcal{T}$hen Jesus told them this parable: "Suppose one of you has a hundred sheep and loses one of them. Does he not leave the ninety-nine in the open country and go after the lost sheep until he finds it? And when he finds it, he joyfully puts it on his shoulders and goes home. Then he calls his friends and neighbors together and says, 'Rejoice with me; I have found my lost sheep.' I tell you that in the same way there will be more rejoicing in heaven over one sinner who repents than over ninety-nine righteous persons who do not need to repent."

—*Luke 15:3–7*

Chapter Six

DOES JESUS CARE?

Jesus—The Good Shepherd

Jesus *does* care for you. To illustrate his compassion, Jesus compared his love to that of a shepherd who would leave ninety-nine sheep in the fold and risk all to search for one that was lost. In the parable of the lost sheep (see Luke 15:3–7), Jesus told of the seeking shepherd who pursued a single sheep until he rescued it and carried it home on his shoulders rejoicing. Paralleling the story of the lost sheep to that of lost humanity, Jesus said, "I tell you that in the same way there will be more rejoicing in heaven over one sinner who repents than over ninety-nine righteous persons who do not need to repent" (v. 7). What a beautiful picture our Lord painted with his words. In this great analogy, he expressed how much he cares for us.

OUR RELATIONSHIP WITH
THE GOOD SHEPHERD IS ONE ON ONE

I have often wondered how a shepherd could know that one specific sheep was missing from the fold. There is no indication in Jesus' parable that the shepherd had to be told that the sheep was missing. No undershepherd announced it to him; he didn't have to count to know one was missing. Rather, our Lord indicated that the shepherd knew each sheep individually; therefore, he knew *which sheep* was missing.

JESUS KNOWS US INDIVIDUALLY

You are not just a number in the mind of God; you are a specific person with individual significance. That fact helps us understand that God cares about us personally. Although Christ came to save the masses of humanity and to die for the whole world, he also came to die for you specifically. And regardless of all our problems, mistakes, and errors, God loves us individually and personally. He knows your name and your needs, and he is prepared to meet the deepest longings of your heart.

I once read a story of a census taker who knocked on the door of a home. When the woman of the house answered the door, the census taker asked her a series of questions. Finally, he asked, "What is the number of your children?" The woman thought for a moment and said, "I don't understand what you mean." The census taker replied, "I need to know the number of your children."

"You must be mistaken, sir," the woman responded. "My children don't have numbers; they have names!"

That is how God regards his children. He calls us all by name. I remember once hearing a little girl saying the Lord's Prayer incorrectly. She got the words wrong, but she got the idea right when she said, "Our Father which art in heaven, how does he know my name?" You will never read in the Bible that God called somebody, "Hey, you." He always called people by their names—Adam, Abraham, Jacob, Moses, Samuel, and Mary. That's the personal touch. The Bible tells us that he even knows the number of the hairs on our head.

Just as Christ knows us individually, so we must also know him individually. He is not just a religious symbol. He is a real person who can be known in an intimate and personal way.

Becoming a Christian Is an Individual Matter

Becoming a Christian is also an individual matter. You are not a Christian just because your parents are Christians. God doesn't have any grandchildren. He accepts us one by one. The fact that your father or mother may be a Christian is irrelevant to whether you are a true believer.

All too often, people think they are Christians because they attend a certain church or belong to a particular denomination. Jesus, himself, made it clear that not all who call him "Lord" are truly saved (see Matthew 7:21–23). He even went so far as to tell Nicodemus, a ruler of the Jews, that he must be born again (see John 3). Our Lord did not commend the ruler's righteous life and urge him to continue on with his good works. Rather, Jesus made it clear to him that his works could not save him apart from spiritual rebirth.

THE GOOD SHEPHERD SEEKS US PERSONALLY

No matter how impersonal the modern world may seem, God is still a personal God, seeking us on an individual basis and calling us to abide under his care.

I have always been impressed by the simple fact that the shepherd in the parable went after the lost sheep himself. He didn't send an assistant or delegate the responsibility to a committee. He didn't even send another shepherd to try it first. He went himself.

Whenever I try to comprehend the simple truth that Christ left heaven for me personally, I am absolutely astounded. Why would the King of Creation leave his throne and be born in a manger to pursue one of his creatures? What advantage was it to him? Why should he leave the glory of heaven to risk all on the cross for me? Yet the greatest fact of history is that Jesus Christ did exactly that. He who had dominion over all powers subjugated himself to human flesh. He could have sent an angel, but he came in person that starry Bethlehem night to claim us for himself.

Someone has said, concerning that night…

> That night when in the Judean skies
> The mystic star dispensed its light,
> A blind man moved in his sleep

And dreamed that he had sight!
That night when shepherds heard the song
Of hosts angelic choiring near,
A deaf man stirred in slumber's spell
And dreamed that he could hear!
That night when in the cattle stall
Slept child and mother cheek by jowl,
A cripple turned his twisted limbs
And dreamed that he was whole!
That night when o'er the newborn babe
The tender Mary rose to lean,
A loathesome leper smiled in sleep
And dreamed that he was clean!
That night when to the mother's heart
The little King was held secure,
A harlot slept a happy sleep
And dreamed that she was pure!
That night when in the manger lay
The sanctified who came to save,
A man moved in the sleep of death
And dreamed there was no grave.

Author Unknown

THE GOOD SHEPHERD LAID DOWN HIS LIFE FOR US

No one else could have accomplished our redemption. Only the sinless Son of God could lay down his life as an acceptable sacrifice for our sins. Only his blood could wash away our iniquity and set us free from the penalty of condemnation we deserved.

In your moments of greatest doubt or personal struggle, you might question whether or not God really loves you. When you find yourself struggling like that, remind yourself that God loved you so much that he sent his Son to die for you personally. Whenever a person lays down his life for someone else, he has done all he could do to prove his love for that person.

When I think of those who gave their lives in Vietnam, Korea, or during World War II, I am amazed at their love and devotion. They gave all they had that we might be free. In a very real sense, they gave their lives for us. Yet some have questioned their integrity and commitment, especially those who fought in Vietnam. I find that hard to understand. Whenever someone lays down his life for others, he or she has given the ultimate measure of devotion.

By the same token, how can anyone question the love of Christ? How can we dare suggest that he does not care for us when he gave his life for us on the cross? He did not die as a martyr or a victim. He died willingly and deliberately in our place. He was not murdered; he laid down his life intentionally. He was not caught in an inescapable series of events. He came into this world to die for our sins and then to triumph over them by his resurrection. The crowd may have called for his crucifixion. The governor may have permitted it. The priests may have demanded it, but Jesus Christ laid down his own life deliberately on our behalf.

$\mathcal{T}$HE GOOD SHEPHERD
CARRIES US HOME

In our Lord's parable about the lost sheep, we notice that the shepherd tenderly picked up the sheep and carried it upon his shoulders. He could have reprimanded it and ordered it home, but he picked it up and carried it home instead.

We have a little apricot poodle named Dusty. Little Dusty is like a member of our family. He even has his own little room in our basement. When we come home and open the door of his room, he comes bounding out, excitedly jumping all over us. We pick him up and hug him because he is dear to our hearts.

It is often said that a dog is a man's best friend. Dusty can't talk back to us. He has never made an ugly remark or an unkind comment to us. He is just a source of unconditional acceptance and joy to all of our family. He is a special little friend.

I can imagine the joy of that little sheep when the shepherd found him. I can picture him, lost, alone, cold, and afraid. I can see him struggling to stay afoot on the craggy mountain ledges. I can see the panic in his eyes as he hears the distant, howling wolves.

The strange thing about sheep is that when they get lost, they become helpless and cannot find their way. They must be sought, or they could be forever lost. In the beauty of our Lord's parable, the shepherd went searching for the sheep and called it to himself.

Jesus said that sheep respond only to the voice of their shepherd, who calls them all by name (see John 10:3). "His sheep follow him," our Lord explained, "because they know his voice" (v. 4). He then announced, "I am the good shepherd. The good shepherd lays down his life for the sheep" (v. 11). He also explained that he knows his sheep, calls his sheep, and gives his life for his sheep. "My sheep listen to my voice; I know them, and they follow me. I give them eternal life, and they shall never perish; no one can snatch them out of my hand," Jesus further explained (vv. 27–28).

Can't you just picture this helpless little lost sheep? Suddenly, he hears the shepherd's voice. *That's my shepherd,* he thinks. Then he bleats out his cry for help. The shepherd hears that little bleat and comes and takes the sheep in his arms. The shepherd holds him close and calms his fears and then hoists him onto his shoulders and carries him home.

Our Lord could not have chosen a more appropriate picture to illustrate his love for us. How could he more vividly tell us to trust him to carry our burdens and bring us safely to heaven? "I will take you just as you are," is what he is implying by this parable. "I will love you and forgive you." Then he puts us on his shoulders and carries us home.

*T*HE GOOD SHEPHERD
KEEPS US SAFE

In the parable of the lost sheep, Jesus said that the shepherd took him *home* to the fold. God does not find us in order to lose us. He does not forgive us and then condemn us. He gives us *eternal* life. The unique quality of that spiritual life is that it lasts forever. It is not eternal one moment and then temporal the next. It lasts forever, and those who have it live forever.

When Christ claims us for himself, he brings us into a permanent and eternal relationship with himself. Once he puts you on his shoulder, he will never let you down. Once you are safe within his fold, you will never be lost again. God's love is unconditional. It is based upon his grace and not our merits. His is not a conditional love that demands that we meet his criteria in order to remain in his fold.

If our security depended on our ability not to fail, we would all be lost. Our security depends upon his power to save us and to sustain us. We can persevere because his Spirit is at work in us.

The gospel, in a nutshell, is stated in John 3:16: "For God so loved the world that he gave his one and only Son, that whoever believes in him shall not perish but have eternal life." *Eternal* is a powerful word. The dictionary describes it as having infinite duration: everlasting. In other words, the salvation that Christ offers us places us safely, securely, and permanently in heaven forever.

This salvation is God's free gift to mankind. He offers it willingly and freely to all who will repent and take it by faith. That is why Jesus said there is joy in heaven "over one sinner who repents" (Luke 15:7). The Bible contains 969 calls to repentance. It is the message of the prophets, of John the Baptist, of Jesus, and of the apostles.

Repent means to "change your mind" (Greek, *metanoeo*) in the New Testament and to "turn" or "change your direction" (Hebrew, *shub*) in the Old Testament. Thus, the full biblical picture of repentance is a change of mind about one's sin, which results in a change of direction in one's life.

❖

Christ, our Shepherd, has left the fold of heaven to seek us among the rocks of this life. When he finds us, he saves us because we cannot save ourselves. He rescues us from destruction and carries us home to heaven.

When we forsake all human effort to save ourselves and cast ourselves on his mercy, we will always find him ready to receive us. It doesn't matter how badly you may have failed, he has succeeded in securing your redemption. It doesn't matter what you may have done wrong, he has done right for you. It doesn't matter who has rejected you, he will accept you, for he is the gentle Shepherd who cares for you!

Healing, in all forms, can only begin when we relinquish control of our lives to Christ. That is the first step. What kind of healing are you seeking? God has proven himself more than capable of helping you. He is our creator, and he understands us better than we do. Can you trust him enough to do his job? Would you allow the Shepherd of your soul to pick you up, hold you close, and take you safely home?

He said to me, "My grace is sufficient for you, for my power is made perfect in weakness." Therefore I will boast all the more gladly about my weaknesses, so that Christ's power may rest on me. That is why, for Christ's sake, I delight in weaknesses, in insults, in hardships, in persecutions, in difficulties. For when I am weak, then I am strong.

—2 Corinthians 12:9–10

Chapter Seven

WHY IS THERE SICKNESS IN THE WORLD?

Sources of Sickness

Almost no one likes to be sick! Americans proved that last year as they consumed more than twenty thousand tons of aspirins in their effort to feel better. No matter how successful you may be in other areas, when you are sick, it is difficult to enjoy life. The desire for physical healing is one of the strongest desires human beings have. When we are not well, we crave wellness. When we are healthy, we hope to continue in good health. But when sickness comes, it is not without significance in the life of the believer.

SOURCES OF SICKNESS

Why do people get sick? What is the source of sickness? Is the source always physical, or are there spiritual sources as well? Sometimes sickness is a result of our own sinful habits and lifestyle; sometimes sickness is an attack from Satan; sometimes it is simply a result of our imperfect physical condition and the aging process; and sometimes sickness is allowed by God to accomplish a greater purpose.

A SINFUL LIFESTYLE

The Bible teaches that our own sin can cause our sickness. What is sin? Sin is "missing the mark." In the word *sin*, the Bible presents the image of an archer missing the mark aimed for. The mark is God's will for our lives. Sin is seen as breaking a commandment, falling short of God's standard of righteousness, or failure to believe God's Word. Sin is ultimately directed against God, which is why it separates us from God. Adam and Eve sinned by breaking God's commandment not to eat of the tree of the knowledge of good and evil. The result was spiritual death, separation from God and the life of God. "But you must not eat from the tree of the knowledge of good and evil, for when you eat of it you will surely die" (Genesis 2:17).

Adam did not die physically the day he sinned—he lived to raise a family—but spiritual death in Adam eventually resulted in his physical death.

Like Adam, our spiritual condition ultimately affects the health of our bodies. Spiritual death, or separation from the life of God, will eventually show up as sickness in the body. The end result of sickness is physical death. Sin is the

cause of spiritual death. "For the wages of sin is death, but
the gift of God is eternal life in Christ Jesus our Lord"
(Romans 6:23).

The apostle Paul understood the connection between sin
and sickness: "That is why many among you are weak and
sick, and a number of you have fallen asleep" (1 Corinthians
11:30). He was writing to the Corinthian believers about
various problems of sin and disobedience in their lives. "That
is why" refers to the sin that had caused many of them to suffer physical illness and had even caused the premature death
of some.

The Destructive Effects of Sin

The real tragedy of sickness resulting from sinful habits
and practices is that it destroys a person physically, mentally, and spiritually. You cannot abuse your body physically
and expect God to simply reverse the destructive process
that you have brought about by your abuse. When that
abuse takes the form of substance abuse, it often affects the
abuser mentally as well. Undoubtedly, the most serious
consequence of all is the spiritual damage that a life of self-
indulgence produces in an individual.

It is not my purpose to specify one form of abuse as nec-
essarily more serious than another. Rather, I am concerned
that you understand that your body is the temple of the
Holy Spirit of God. It *does* make a difference what you do
with your body and what you put into your body, because
your body belongs to God. We cannot permanently forestall

the aging process in our lives, but we certainly have an obligation not to speed it up.

A Spiritual Solution Is Needed for Spiritual Sickness

If you are sick, look more deeply for spiritual explanations for the illness and for recovery. Your sickness could be a physical symptom of an underlying spiritual condition. Physical and psychological therapies treat only the symptoms but leave the root cause unaddressed. Similarly, the ancient Jews covered their sin with the blood of bulls and goats. A physical sacrifice was made, but the sin remained. A spiritual sacrifice was required to take away their sin and our sins. This sacrifice was the blood of Christ.

A spiritual remedy is needed to permanently eradicate sickness—whether of the mind or the body.

Have you ever noticed that men of God, including Jesus, often gave the sick a task to complete—one that often appeared impossible—and if they would obey, they would be healed? Naaman had to dip seven times in the Jordan. The man with the shriveled hand had to stretch it out. The paralyzed man had to pick up his mat and walk. The blind man had to wash in the pool of Siloam. The man crippled from birth had to stand upright on his feet. Why were these acts often required? To understand fully, you have to remember that disobedience and unbelief are equivalent in the Bible. We know that the opposite is also true, faith and righteousness are interchangeable. "Abram believed the LORD; and he credited it to him as righteousness" (Genesis 15:6).

Consider this: *If one act of sin, disobedience, or unbelief, can result in sickness, then one act of righteousness, obedience, or faith can result in healing.* This is true for the whole church corporately as well as for us individually.

> Consequently, just as the result of one trespass was con-demnation for all men, so also the result of one act of righteousness was justification that brings life for all men. For just as through the disobedience of the one man the many were made sinners, so also through the obedience of the one man the many will be made righteous. (Romans 5:18–19)

Remember in chapter 3 when we wrote about forgive-ness being one of the three steps for emotional healing? Well, it stands to reason that if sin can result in sickness, forgiveness can result in healing. Jesus, the man without sin, has paid the penalty of death so that our sin could be per-manently done away with and forgiveness could be ours.

His physical body was broken so that our bodies could be healed. "Surely he took up our infirmities and carried our sorrows, yet we considered him stricken by God, and smit-ten by him, and afflicted. But he was pierced for our trans-gressions, he was crushed for our iniquities; the punishment that brought us peace was upon him, and by his wounds we are healed" (Isaiah 53:4–5).

The Hebrew word translated "infirmities" in Isaiah 53:4 means malady, calamity, *disease*, or *sickness*. The Hebrew word translated "sorrows" in the same verse means sorrow, anguish, or *pain*. Many people argue that this verse refers to "spiritual healing," but Matthew would disagree. "When

❖

evening came, many who were demon-possessed were brought to him, and he drove out the spirits with a word and healed all the sick. This was to fulfill what was spoken through the prophet Isaiah: 'He took up our *infirmities* and carried our *diseases*'" (Matthew 8:16–17, emphasis added).

If sickness originates in an act of sin on our part, then the possibility for healing begins when we receive forgiveness for that sin:

> Is any one of you sick? He should call the elders of the church to pray over him and anoint him with oil in the name of the Lord. And the prayer offered in faith will make the sick person well; the Lord will raise him up. If he has sinned, he will be forgiven. Therefore, confess your sins to each other and pray for each other so that you may be healed. The prayer of a righteous man is powerful and effective. (James 5:14–16)

Thank God, we have an advocate with the Father who can be touched with the feeling of our infirmities.

An Attack from Satan

In the story of Job we certainly see that Satan put his hand against Job to cause both calamity and physical illness in his life. While God set a limit on the extent of Satan's ability to inflict this illness on Job, God nevertheless allowed Satan to do it. The Bible says, "So Satan went out from the presence of the LORD and afflicted Job with painful sores" (Job 2:7). Job was suffering, not because of sin in his own personal life, but because Satan had afflicted him. Now that doesn't mean that all sickness is a direct result of

Satan's activity, but this passage makes it clear that in some cases it certainly is.

OUR IMPERFECT BODIES AND THE AGING PROCESS

I know this may come as a surprise to you, but your body is not perfect. And not only that, the world you were born into is not perfect. Inherent in this earth and in your body are sickness and death, germs and weakness. You were not intended to live in this realm forever. Much sickness in this world is simply a result of the kind of creatures we are and the kind of world we live in. Every day, people get colds and infections; every day, people weaken and die.

And to make matters worse, our imperfect bodies also succumb to the effects of aging. The older we get, the closer we come to death. Our bodies are in the process of aging every single day. We may try to camouflage that process or cover it up, but it continues unabated. We can dye our hair, buy a wig, get a face-lift, or tuck in our tummy, but the truth is we are still getting older. I recently read an article stating that due to the advances in medicine, the five stages of adulthood are changing. You may not be as old as you think! They are now categorized as:

Emerging Adults—18–30 years old
Young Adults—30–50 years old
Middle Adults—50–70 years old
Senior Adults—70–80 years old
Elderly Adults—80+ years old

I like the way this author counts it! But in reality,

regardless of what category you find yourself in, illness will catch up with you one day, and you will eventually die. The Bible says very clearly, "Man is destined to die once" (Hebrews 9:27). Unless Christ returns in our lifetime, we all have an appointment with death. You may not like thinking about it, but it is an ever-encroaching reality that must be faced. For the majority of people, sickness and death come as a result of our imperfect bodies and the aging process.

❖

SICKNESS MAY BE ALLOWED TO ACCOMPLISH GOD'S PURPOSES

Once again, we look to the apostle Paul for insight on physical sickness. Read how he viewed his own physical impairment:

> To keep me from becoming conceited because of these surpassingly great revelations, there was given me a thorn in my flesh, a messenger of Satan, to torment me. Three times I pleaded with the Lord to take it away from me. But he said to me, "My grace is sufficient for you, for my power is made perfect in weakness." Therefore I will boast all the more gladly about my weaknesses, so that Christ's power may rest on me. That is why, for Christ's sake, I delight in weaknesses, in insults, in hardships, in persecutions, in difficulties. For when I am weak, then I am strong. (2 Corinthians 12:7–10)

The depth of truth expressed by Paul in this one passage is more than adequate to help us face the problem of physical illness. There is little doubt that Paul's "thorn in [the] flesh" was a physical illness. He explained that this sickness was being used by Satan to "torment" him, meaning that Satan was attempting to discourage Paul and beat down his spirit. Yet through it all, God used this illness to produce genuine humility and an unbelievable level of spiritual maturity in his servant Paul. God's answer to Paul was to point him to his "sufficient" grace, which would enable Paul not only to endure the suffering but to use it for God's glory.

Paul did not take the attitude that this "thorn" did not bother him; rather, he made it clear that he was distressed by it. But at the same time, Paul realized that God was at work in his life to bring about his divine purpose.

Job is another example of how God allows sickness to accomplish his divine purpose. God used Job to prove a point to Satan: Some of his followers do not serve him only when life is good; the best ones serve him even in the midst of horrible suffering.

From Job we learn another truth: God set a limit on what he would allow Satan to do and demanded that he not take Job's life. This truth assures us that if we are suffering as a believer, we can rest assured that God will not allow us to suffer beyond the point he has set.

*O*UR GOOD GOD
DESIRES OUR GOOD

Our God is a good God: "And, behold, one came and said unto him, Good Master, what good thing shall I do, that I may have eternal life? And he said unto him, Why callest thou me good? there is none good but one, that is, God" (Matthew 19:16–17 KJV).

What is the meaning of the word *good?* God's character is its definition. His character is reflected in the fruit of the Spirit: "But the fruit of the Spirit is love, joy, peace, patience, kindness, goodness, faithfulness, gentleness and self-control. Against such things there is no law" (Galatians 5:22–23).

What would it benefit humans if God had the knowledge and the power to heal but not the desire? We are guaranteed that by his very nature, it is his will to heal. The character of God matches all his other qualities—his omniscience and his omnipotence.

Most humans, unlike God, become more oppressive and abusive as they acquire more authority and power. But God, who *is* all power, came to the earth "to serve and to give his life as a ransom for many" (Matthew 20:28). No power restrains God from doing anything he chooses, yet he chooses to love and to bless.

The goodness of God exceeds our ability to comprehend. Who has ever plumbed the depths of God's love? Our God is love!

> Who shall separate us from the love of Christ? Shall trouble or hardship or persecution or famine or nakedness or danger or sword? As it is written: "For your sake we face death all day long; we are considered as sheep to be slaughtered." No, in all these things we are more than conquerors through him who loved us. For I am convinced that neither death nor life, neither angels nor

demons, neither the present nor the future, nor any powers, neither height nor depth, nor anything else in all
creation, will be able to separate us from the love of God
that is in Christ Jesus our Lord. (Romans 8:35–39)

One day Moses asked God to show him his glory. "'Now
show me your glory.' And the LORD said, 'I will cause all my
goodness to pass in front of you, and I will proclaim my
name, the LORD, in your presence'" (Exodus 33:18–19).
The Hebrew word for *glory* means heavy or weighty. What
Moses was really asking was to see the heaviest or weightiest
thing about God—his very essence. So God let his *goodness*
pass before him.

It is *good* to relieve pain and suffering, to restore health,
or to reunite a husband and wife or a mother and child.
When Peter healed the man crippled from birth at the gate
called Beautiful, the Holy Ghost called it a "good deed."

Then Peter, filled with the Holy Ghost, said unto them, Ye
rulers of the people, and elders of Israel, if we this day be
examined of the *good deed* done to the impotent man, by
what means he is made whole; Be it known unto you all,
and to all the people of Israel, that by the name of Jesus
Christ of Nazareth, whom ye crucified, whom God raised
from the dead, even by him doth this man stand here
before you whole. (Acts 4:8–10 KJV, emphasis added)

Peter did not even heal that man; Jesus did. And Jesus
continues to do good today. Jesus isn't dead! His ministry
never ceases. Jesus is God. If you want to understand what
good is, watch Jesus.

When Peter preached to Cornelius and to those

gathered with him, he said, "You know...how God anointed Jesus of Nazareth with the Holy Spirit and power, and how he went around doing good and healing all who were under the power of the devil, because God was with him" (Acts 10:37–38). Jesus went around "doing good and healing." One thing is clear: Jesus did not heal only to prove his divinity; Jesus healed because of his great compassion. He couldn't help himself. It is God's very nature to heal and nurture, to love and comfort. To do otherwise would be to deny his very self.

So then, what is a person to do when they get sick? Read on.

Therefore, since we have a great high priest who has gone through the heavens, Jesus the Son of God, let us hold firmly to the faith we profess. For we do not have a high priest who is unable to sympathize with our weaknesses, but we have one who has been tempted in every way, just as we are—yet was without sin. Let us then approach the throne of grace with confidence, so that we may receive mercy and find grace to help us in our time of need.

—*Hebrews 4:14–16*

Chapter Eight

WHY DOESN'T GOD HEAL ALL WHO ASK?

Seven Steps for Seeking Healing

Jesus' ministry on earth certainly teaches us that Jesus Christ has power to deliver us from any sin, sickness, or disease. He is the Almighty God and the Creator of everything. In fact, Scripture tells us that everything is held together by the power of Jesus. If he created our bodies, then he certainly can heal our bodies if he chooses. Describing his own ministry, Jesus said, "The Spirit of the Lord is on me, because he has anointed me to preach good news to the poor. He has sent me to proclaim freedom for the prisoners and recovery of sight for the blind, to release the oppressed, to proclaim the year of the Lord's favor" (Luke 4:18–19).

Is Jesus in the ministry of deliverance? Absolutely! Consistently, we see Jesus healing and restoring people physically, spiritually, and emotionally. And he desires to

CHAPTER

$\mathcal{8}$

❖

104

heal us today just as he did in his earthly ministry two thousand years ago. Does he have the power to heal? Indeed he does—and he has the power to heal all manner of diseases. Is anything too hard for God? Nothing!

I am often asked, "Pastor, do you believe God can heal the sick and afflicted?" I respond, "Certainly, for do we not have his word on it?" I have seen his healing power in my own body. I have also seen his healing power in the lives of many others.

From childhood, I have been exposed to the healing power of God. I recall the days of the sawdust tent meetings in the late '50s and early '60s, when I was a boy. We would witness times when thousands of people would come together praying for a moving of God. Those days and times are totally unknown today. The people of those days were full of expectation and had a simple faith in the power of God. When there are that many folks gathered with that kind of faith, something is sure to happen. Normally it did!

It was a time in my life I shall not forget—a time I saw God's power at work in the lives of many! Were folks really healed of sickness in those meetings? Without a doubt they were, and when it happened, the thousands who were there would rejoice and applaud in praise to the Lord. Yet others, I'm sorry to say, would not be healed. They would silently walk away.

During my boyhood, I saw many such meetings with many different evangelists and many different prayer lines for the sick. Yet even as a child, I wondered: *If God can heal,*

why doesn't he heal them all? Doesn't he care about everybody?
And what about me? If I need him, will he love me enough to
heal me? Over the years, I have learned that each one of us
must trust God for our own healing.

$\mathcal{A}$ STORY
OF HEALING

Let's look at the story found in Matthew 8:5–13 about
the miracle of the healing of the servant of a Roman centurion to see if we can better understand how to appropriate
healing in our lives.

The story opens when Jesus entered Capernaum, on the
northwest shore of Galilee. Jesus was frequently seen here
with his disciples or with a crowd. Capernaum is believed to
have been his primary resting place during his Galilean
ministry. Jesus had been speaking to a crowd, expounding
on doctrines and teaching the people.

While there, a centurion approached him and caught his
attention. Roman soldiers were commonplace in Capernaum
at this time. The city was a seaport and customs station.
Many affluent officers of the Roman government lived there.
It was also occupied by the Roman soldiers whose job was to
keep the Jews content by erecting a synagogue in the city.

This particular centurion frantically came to Jesus, begging him, "Lord, my servant lies at home paralyzed and in terrible suffering" (v. 6). Jesus responded by simply saying to the
man, "I will go and heal him" (v. 7). To this, the centurion
responded that he was not worthy to have Jesus in his home

Why

Doesn't

God Heal

All Who

Ask?

❖

105

and that if Jesus would just say the words, his servant would be healed. He then explained that he understood the principles of authority. Just as a commander in the Roman army, all Jesus had to do was speak and the instruction would be carried out. The centurion believed that Jesus' authority included the ability to heal people of disease. Jesus was amazed at this man's faith, and he looked to the disciples and said, "I tell you the truth, I have not found anyone in Israel with such great faith" (v. 10).

SEVEN STEPS TO FOLLOW WHEN SEEKING HEALING

If you are presently suffering from physical illness in your life, let me suggest seven steps for dealing with that sickness. To aid our discussion, we'll further examine the story of healing we just discussed.

STEP #1: COME TO JESUS WITH YOUR NEED

This first point may seem obvious, but many overlook it. If we need healing, we must come to Jesus with our need. The Roman centurion's first step was coming to Jesus; this showed that he believed Jesus could meet his need. We see over and over in the Bible that we need to come to Jesus in order to receive help. Jesus himself said, "Come to me, all you who are weary and burdened, and I will give you rest" (Matthew 11:28) and "Whoever comes to me I will never drive away" (John 6:37). In other instances of healing, people came to Jesus with their needs, and he healed them.

In fact, most instances of healing occurred when people *came to Jesus* and *sought him out* with their needs. We should not ignore this precedent; we, also, should approach him with our needs. Hebrews 4:16 specifically instructs us to come boldly to God's throne of grace so that we can obtain help in our times of need. When we come to Jesus with our needs, we demonstrate our trust and our faith in his ability to meet that need.

Why

Doesn't

God Heal

All Who

Ask?

❖

107

STEP #2: REQUEST—DON'T DEMAND

Next, we notice that the centurion came with a *request* for Christ to heal his servant, not with a demand. He approached with a humble attitude, aware of the fact that Jesus' authority gave him the right to deny the request. We need to understand that God's sovereignty gives him the right to choose how he will respond. We cannot manipulate God; we can only come to him with a humble attitude and believe that he can overcome our situation. Respecting his sovereignty should also make us mindful that our demands cannot accomplish anything. And just as the centurion humbled himself to beg Jesus' assistance on behalf of his servant, so should we humble ourselves.

Now you may say, "I would never demand anything from Jesus." But so often we do. We know what our problem is and have even figured out how God should fix it. We pray, saying, "God, I have this problem. Now if you will do things this way, I won't have this problem." Does that sound familiar? We do this so often and never realize how demanding we are of God.

The major problem with this technique is that it does not work! Why? Because we ignore that the will of God is to do what is best for his children. God knows more than we do, and he understands what we need, even before we need it. Jesus lovingly calls us to cast our cares upon him, for he cares for us. He simply says, "Let me have them; I know what is best for you." The centurion came to Christ demanding nothing; rather, he simply trusted that the God who made his servant could heal his servant if he wished.

Step #3: Submit to God's Authority

When we bring our requests to Jesus, we come in obedience to his authority. The centurion demonstrated this obedience when he responded, "Lord, I do not deserve to have you come under my roof. But just say the word, and my servant will be healed. For I myself am a man under authority, with soldiers under me. I tell this one, 'Go,' and he goes; and that one, 'Come,' and he comes. I say to my servant, 'Do this,' and he does it" (Matthew 8:8–9).

This soldier was a man of authority! He was a Roman centurion, given charge of one hundred fighting soldiers. He would have been one of sixty men in charge of a Roman legion. His responsibilities would have included drilling his men; inspecting their weapons, food, and clothing; and commanding them in battle. If men did not obey his orders, they could be killed on the spot. A centurion held complete authority over the soldiers. This man knew well the power of the spoken word. When he spoke, it was with the authority and power of Rome behind him. His explanation of authority was to show Jesus that he understood his power. He recognized that Jesus was Creator and under the authority of heaven itself.

It is useless to ask God for anything unless we are willing to live under his authority. We must do what he tells us to do—without compromise—when he tells us to do it, no matter what it may be! This is the only way to truly live under the authority of God. If we do not submit ourselves, we might as well not ask.

I believe that one of the reasons few people are healed today is that few are willing to submit to God's authority. They want the blessings of God but do not want the responsibility of walking closely with him and living in total obedience to his will.

The old hymn "Trust and Obey" describes it so aptly:

> Then in fellowship sweet, we will sit at His feet,
> Or we'll walk by His side in the way;
> What He says we will do, where He sends we will go.
> Never fear, only trust and obey.
> Trust and obey, for there's no other way
> To be happy in Jesus, but to trust and obey.

STEP #4: BELIEVE THAT IT CAN BE DONE!

The last principle that we see in this story is that we need to have the faith that God *can* work and *will* work in our situation. What impressed Jesus about the centurion was his faith: "He was astonished and said…, 'I have not found anyone in Israel with such great faith'" (v. 10). Jesus went on to say that many "from the east and the west" would take their places in the kingdom of God. This man would be one of those men of faith. And true to the man's faith, Jesus simply spoke the words and Scripture tells us that the servant was healed at that very same moment. "'Go! It will be done just as you believed it would.' And his servant was healed at that very hour" (v. 13).

Just as this man believed and asked God, we must do the same. Although we do not have the opportunity to find Jesus walking along our streets, he has provided a means to communicate with him. Philippians 4:6 tells us that through our prayers, we need to make our requests known to God, not being anxious or fearful. We should not be surprised when God answers our prayers, as long as we approach him with a pure heart and have the faith to believe that he can work miraculously in our lives. So often we pray but do not believe that God wants to answer our prayers or is capable of answering our prayers. This man staked it all on Jesus and wasn't surprised when the answer came.

A Biblical Example of Faith in Action

In Acts 12, we see a different picture of prayer and a lack of belief that God is listening and actively working. Peter has been thrown into prison during the Passover season because Herod became hostile toward the church in Jerusalem. Herod had recently murdered James, the brother of John the apostle. Peter's life was spared for the moment because it was Passover time. Herod intended to bring Peter before the Jews, most likely to be killed like James, because it would please them. Peter was under heavy guard and bound hand and foot. He slept between soldiers, and a guard was at the door. This would have weighed heavily on Peter's mind as he sat in the prison, even as he prayed for deliverance.

Several believers from the church had gathered in prayer for Peter at the house of John Mark's mother—and God responded. He sent an angel to Peter's cell during the night. The angelic visitor awakened Peter and removed his chains. He then told Peter to put on his clothes and shoes and to follow him. The angel led him into the city, down the streets, right to Mary's door. All this time, Peter "had no idea that what the angel was doing was really happening" (v. 9). But when the angel left him, he knew that God had delivered him out of the hands of Herod and the Jews. When he realized that he was standing in front of Mary's house, he knocked on the door and a young girl named Rhoda came and asked who it was. Peter responded, and Rhoda, recognizing his voice, turned and ran to tell the others that Peter was standing at the door! Instead of believing that God had done what they were asking, they told her to be quiet and would not believe her. When she

Why

Doesn't

God Heal

All Who

Ask?

❖

111

kept insisting, they suggested that it was his angel at the door. But this did not stop Rhoda, who knew for a fact that God answered their prayers. The Bible says that Peter continued to knock, and when they finally opened the door, they were "astonished" to see Peter. Astonished at answered prayer! If God miraculously answered our prayers, would we be surprised? How often do we pray and not truly expect a response? God calls us to pray with faith, not doubt. If we pray without faith, we seldom see the results.

Why Is Faith So Important?

The Scripture clearly teaches that we can come to God by faith and request physical healing. We must not demand it from God, but we can come boldly before the throne of grace and call upon Jesus for his healing touch.

But what is so special about faith? It permeates the pages of the Word of God from Genesis to Revelation. It is the essential ingredient in any exchange between God and man. In fact, Scripture says that we cannot please God without it: "Without faith it is impossible to please God, because anyone who comes to him must believe that he exists and that he rewards those who earnestly seek him" (Hebrews 11:6). By our faith we gain access into the "grace in which we now stand" (Romans 5:2). Deliverance from sin and sickness and all the power of the enemy is by faith.

Faith is equivalent to obedience and righteousness: "To the man who does not work but trusts God who justifies the wicked, his faith is credited as righteousness" (Romans 4:5).

What Is Healing Faith?

Faith is the heart cry of the child of God. It penetrates the heavens, parting the veil, allowing us to obtain all the will of the Father. It is a light the darkness cannot extinguish, an anchor the storm has no power to uproot.

Faith sees the invisible, believes the unthinkable, and does the impossible. Faith is the life of the righteous, the substance of intangible hope, the assurance of possession in the absence of perception. Faith proceeds seeing, hearing, touching. Believing is seeing! The writer of Hebrews says, "Now faith is being sure of what we hope for and certain of what we do not see" (Hebrews 11:1). What does Scripture teach about the characteristics of faith? Plenty.

Faith is fully persuaded. Speaking of Abraham, Scripture says, "He did not waiver through unbelief regarding the promise of God, but was strengthened in his faith and gave glory to God, being fully persuaded that God had power to do what he had promised" (Romans 4:20–21). The Book of James says we must not doubt: "When he asks, he must believe and not doubt, because he who doubts is like a wave of the sea, blown and tossed by the wind. That man should not think he will receive anything from the Lord; he is a double-minded man, unstable in all he does" (1:6–8).

Faith trusts in the character of our God and in the veracity of his Word. Faith defines truth by eternal standards. It is a gift from the Father to the heart of the believer. The psalmist knew what it meant to trust in the unfailing character of

Why

Doesn't

God Heal

All Who

Ask?

❖

113

God: "But I trust in your unfailing love; my heart rejoices in your salvation" (Psalm 13:5).

Faith is never stagnant; it should be ever increasing, fed on the holy Scriptures and exercised in the trials of life. Paul praised the Thessalonians for their increasing faith: "We ought always to thank God for you, brothers, and rightly so, because your faith is growing more and more, and the love every one of you has for each other is increasing" (2 Thessalonians 1:3).

Faith gives glory to God in advance of evidence. Like Paul in prison, it sings praises at midnight, ignoring the chains that bind and worships in the day of adversity. It looks beyond the storm-swept sea to meet the Master's eyes, and it walks upon the living rock of his Word.

Faith has a voice! " 'The word is near you; it is in your mouth and in your heart,' that is, the word of faith we are proclaiming" (Romans 10:8).

Faith flows from the heart through the mouth and frames new worlds of beauty conceived in heaven. It calls things that are not as though they were, and they become. It calls defeat victory and weakness strength.

David believed and spoke, and the giant perished. Joshua believed and spoke, and the walls crumbled. Abel believed, and now by faith, though he is dead, he still speaks. If you have ears to hear, you can yet hear his words echoing through the ages. Faith has the ring of immortality to it. It speaks of higher thoughts and higher ways. Through us, Abraham's faith is still reaping the promise.

Faith's voice speaks the language of truth, the vocabulary of blessing, the dialect of peace. No lie is found on its holy lips.

Faith combs God's Word for the promises of God. Then with the lips it turns the key; with the tongue of thanksgiving, it slides the bolt; and with actions in harmony with its words, it opens the door. What faith has opened, no man can shut.

Faith demands action. Noah built the ark. Abraham offered Isaac. David ran to meet the giant. Their faith and their actions were working together. Their actions quickened their faith. The Roman centurion we discussed earlier had a great faith mixed with a great obedience, and that brought great power with God. And Jesus rewarded his display of faith by answering his request to heal his servant.

Faith must be exercised. James 2:14 says, "What good is it, my brothers, if a man claims to have faith but has no deeds?" Use your faith or lose your faith! Feed it with the Word. Water it with the Spirit. Exercise it, embrace it, and protect it—for your faith is your victory!

God wants us to come to him in faith and ask for his intervention on our behalf. But he doesn't guarantee healing based upon the degree of our faith. The healing response of God is conditional upon two factors: our faith and his will.

STEP #5: ADD PATIENCE TO YOUR FAITH

Through faith and patience, you inherit the promises. Make up your mind never to quit! The darker it gets, the

Why

Doesn't

God Heal

All Who

Ask?

❖

115

more you confess. The longer it takes, the stronger you become. How long do you have to do it? For as long as it takes. Every case is different. Healing can take ten days, six weeks, three years, or longer. In some cases, it may not come this side of heaven, but rest assured, healing will come. Just decide in your heart right now that you're in it for the long haul, and come hell or high water, you will never quit. Once you are locked in to faith, your victory is assured. The only way you can lose is by agreeing to be defeated, so refuse to agree!

When I was a teenager, there was a lady in our church named Mrs. Epps. This dear lady had an unusually large tumor on the side of her neck. Each Wednesday night, our church gathered for prayer and testimony. This was a time for all who wished to give a personal testimony about what God had done for them the past week. Each Wednesday night, this dear lady would stand and say the same thing she had said the week before, "I thank the Lord for answering my prayer and healing my neck of this tumor."

When she would say that, I'm sure most folks wondered if she were mentally stable. Couldn't she see that the tumor was still there? Wasn't it foolish to thank God for her deliverance before it happened? Well, one Wednesday night when testimony time came, Mrs. Epps stood and gave the same testimony, "I thank the Lord for answering my prayer and healing my neck of this tumor"—only this time, the tumor *was gone!* Completely gone! Everyone else was amazed and excited that this obvious healing had taken place, but Mrs. Epps had the same demeanor and attitude she'd always had. I've often thought of this woman as a true demonstration of the essence of faith. She lived out 1 John 5:14–15: "This is the confidence we have in approaching God: that if we ask anything according to his will, he hears us. And if we know that he hears us—whatever we ask—we know that we have what we asked of him."

Why

Doesn't

God Heal

All Who

Ask?

❖

117

STEP #6: CONFESS AND FORSAKE ALL KNOWN SIN

As we have seen, there are many reasons why people are sick. In some cases, it is merely a result of the frailty of our bodies and the aging process. For others, sickness is an attack of Satan. (But in every "attack" case, God, in his goodness, sets a limit on that suffering and overrules it for his own good purpose.) And sometimes, God allows sickness to bring about his divine purpose. But for some, sickness is a direct result of a sinful lifestyle.

If you are in need of healing, examine your heart to make sure that your suffering is not a result of some deliberate sin in your life. If you do have such sin in your life, confess it to God and forsake it. If you are ill because of a destructive habit that is destroying your physical body, you may not be able to undo all of the damage that has been done, but the sooner you quit, the better. Without making a complete break from that habit, you may never know the kind of health that you could have known had you quit.

You can continue to go through the routine of life pretending that your illness is not all that serious. But chances are that it will eventually take you. There is nothing more tragic than a premature death caused by a sinful habit that was known to be harmful but was never dealt with. The psalmist put it like this, "Before I was afflicted I went astray, but now I obey your word" (Psalm 119:67). The writer acknowledged that his sinful lifestyle had led him astray and resulted in physical illness. But he had now come to a point of physical repentance and had returned to the Lord and was keeping his commandments.

The longer you indulge in sinful habits, the more you will accelerate the process of sickness and death in your own body. The sooner you turn away from those habits, the more quickly you can hope to return to health.

Step #7: Trust God to Do What Is Best for You

There is a vast difference between trusting the sovereignty of God and fatalistically resigning oneself to sickness without hope of change. For example, if you have been told that you have cancer, you can resign yourself to the consequences and sit there and die, or you can make use of every possible medical procedure to help cure the cancer and pray in faith asking God to heal you. I believer the latter option is the correct one.

All of us have seen many who received healing through prayer and medicine working hand in hand. With that in mind, the essence of the prayer of the believer should be something like this:

Dear Lord, I know that you love me more than I love myself. I believe that your purposes for my life are greater than my own could ever be. Therefore, I believe you will answer my prayer in the greatest way possible. I am asking you to heal me of this sickness. By faith, I thank you in advance for hearing my prayer and bringing me the answer. I receive my healing in accordance to your will. In the mighty name of Jesus Christ, I pray. Amen.

When you pray like that, you will have come to a point of spiritual maturity where you are able to trust the sovereign purpose of God, while at the same time believing that he can move miraculously on your behalf. By taking these seven steps toward healing, the outcome will always be the very best God has for you. And you can firmly place your trust in that unfailing truth!

Why

Doesn't

God Heal

All Who

Ask?

❖

119

In those days Hezekiah became ill and was at the point of death. The prophet Isaiah son of Amoz went to him and said, "This is what the LORD says: Put your house in order, because you are going to die; you will not recover."

Hezekiah turned his face to the wall and prayed to the LORD, "Remember, O LORD, how I have walked before you faithfully and with wholehearted devotion and have done what is good in your eyes." And Hezekiah wept bitterly.

Then the word of the LORD came to Isaiah: "Go and tell Hezekiah, 'This is what the LORD, the God of your father David, says: I have heard your prayer and seen your tears; I will add fifteen years to your life.'"

—*Isaiah 38:1–5*

Chapter Nine

CAN HUMANS
CHANGE GOD'S MIND?
Pleading Your Case before God

To have a sentence of death pronounced against you would be a terrible thing. None of us wants to die right now. Regardless of your opinion of the man, comedian Woody Allen had it right when he said, "I don't mind dying all that much. I just don't want to be there when it happens."

As a pastor I have been with numerous people when the doctor pronounced a sentence of death upon them. I've heard words like, "I'm sorry, but we've done all we can. As much as we would like to tell you otherwise, it seems that you have only a short time to live." I've seen the shock and sadness of such pronouncements; they are hard to bear regardless of how gently they are handled. But, are such words always true? Is death sure to come to pass the way and time it is pronounced? Let's find out from an account in the Bible.

Isaiah 38 tells the story of Good King Hezekiah. Unlike his wicked father, Ahab, Hezekiah was a good man who sought to please the Lord his God. One day he was visited at the palace by his friend, Isaiah the prophet. Isaiah brought him a message from none other than God himself. The message was clear and to the point: "Hezekiah," he said, "This is what the LORD says: Put your house in order, for you are going to die; you will not recover" (v. 1). What a thought! Suddenly, unexpectedly, this good king of Judah had his world turned upside down. The ultimate sentence, the sentence of death, had been passed upon him. Not by a medical doctor or nurse but by God himself.

*H*EZEKIAH PLED HIS CASE
BEFORE GOD

What was Hezekiah to do? Did he simply throw up his hands and quit. Did he just say, "All right, God, go ahead. I'll just die." Not at all! In fact, the Bible says that he actually found a way to move the hand of God on his own behalf. And instead of letting him die, God added fifteen wonderful years to his life.

Let's take a look at the events surrounding this man who defeated the sentence of death and see the steps that he took to bring about this incredible miracle.

He Turned His Face toward God

After Isaiah told Hezekiah that he would die, the Scripture tells us that he "turned his face to the wall and prayed to the LORD" (v. 2). That means that he got his focus off of everything and everybody but God. The sentence of death would bring us to that, don't you think? The focus of life becomes a great deal more narrow when we find that our days are numbered. Hezekiah had come to the place in his life when he understood that if God would not help him, no one would.

Spiritual focus is an all important thing. If we are asking God for healing, and if the focus of our life is on everything except him, how serious will he take our request? As you read this today, may I ask you a question? Where is God in your list of priorities? Is he at the top of your focus list? Have you made him Lord of all? If so, then you have taken the first step in your healing. Helen Lemmel had it right when she wrote:

> Turn your eyes upon Jesus
> Look full in His wonderful face,
> And the things of earth
> Will grow strangely dim,
> In the light of His glory and grace.

He Argued His Case before God

The prophet had said, "You are going to die," but Hezekiah said, "Remember, O LORD, how I have walked

Can

Humans

Change

God's

Mind?

❖

123

before you faithfully and with wholehearted devotion and have done what is good in your eyes" (v. 3). He prayed in desperation, pleading his case before the throne of God in heaven.

There is an interesting scripture several chapters later in the Book of Isaiah. It tells us that we can argue our case before God. Through the prophet, God speaks: "Review the past for me, let us argue the matter together; state the case for your innocence" (43:26). Charles Finney, the great revivalist, said, "Argumentative prayers are the best kind of praying." Does that mean that we actually "argue" with God as we think of arguing today? Of course not! It simply means that we should clearly, plainly, explicitly, with our whole heart and full of conviction, state our case to him.

Now how is that done? Let us imagine how a lawyer would do it. First, to properly present a case, we must *plan for it*. By this, I mean that our prayers to God can be planned in such a way that they will make sense. Hezekiah gave three reasons for God's mercy to be granted to him. He said, "Remember, O LORD,... [1] I have walked before you faithfully... [2] with wholehearted devotion and [3] have done ...good in your eyes." That is planned praying.

Second, we should *prepare*. The preparation occurs in our hearts. Was Hezekiah a perfect man? Of course not; no one is perfect! He was not claiming perfection, just that his heart with "wholehearted devotion" belonged to God. That is not perfection; that is trusting in the perfection of God alone. Doubtless the king had taken inventory of his soul and settled his account with God. Therefore, he could speak to God knowing that he was prepared to enter into his presence. We must prepare ourselves through confession, repentance, and acceptance of God's forgiveness before we can rightfully plead our case before him.

I have in my office a calculator. I use it often in the daily activities of our busy church and broadcast ministries. Recently, I had an exceptionally long list of figures that I had to add. In fact, I had entered so many numbers that after about thirty minutes it seemed as if my fingers were numb! Then suddenly, because of my tired hands, I hit the button with the letter C on it. *Pow!* In a flash, all that I had done was gone. Everything I tried to do to retrieve it was in vain. It was over—finished—never to be seen again. Sitting back in my chair, I thought, *That is what God does with the record of our sins.* They are added up against us. The list gets longer and longer, if we let it. But when we come to the cross of Christ in repentance and acceptance of his forgiveness—pow! In a flash, all the wrong that we have done is gone forever! Over. Finished. Never to be seen again. Preparation means that we prepare our hearts.

Finally, we *present* our case to God in prayer. We tell him how our heart feels and why we feel as we do. God is expecting us to tell him. He has promised that in Christ Jesus we have a high priest who is able to sympathize with our weaknesses (see Hebrews 4:15). God is not cold. His heart is warmed with love and compassion and is touched when we bring our prayers and petitions to him. So we come boldly

Can

Humans

Change

God's

Mind?

❖

125

before his throne, bringing our petitions into his presence, fully expecting his mercy and healing touch to be ours.

HE PRAYED WITH A HUMBLE SPIRIT

The king realized that with all he had, he had nothing without God. He was the sovereign king of the nation of Judah—rich, strong, powerful, and popular. If anyone had a reason for pride, Hezekiah did. Yet, the scriptures tell us that he "wept bitterly" before God. His heart was humbled and broken before the Lord. Access to the throne room of heaven was granted because of his humility. God loves a broken and contrite heart, we are told (see Psalm 51:17). Why? Because humility is the opposite of pride, and pride is one of the root causes of sin. Satan fell from heaven because of pride, and God has resisted it since that very day.

If we think of ourselves in self-righteousness, pointing out to God in pride what we have done for him, we've missed the point of it all. Spiritual pride and self-righteousness is not only foolish, it is spiritual suicide with God. The Bible teaches us that God resists the proud but gives his abundant grace to the humble (see James 4:6). Hezekiah came with a heart that was broken in humility. God saw it, and it pleased him.

GOD MOVED HIS HEALING HAND

The great mercy of the Lord is recorded in Isaiah 38:4–5: "Then the word of the LORD came to Isaiah: 'Go and tell Hezekiah, "This is what the LORD, the God of your father David, says: I have heard your prayer and seen your tears; I will add fifteen years to your life." '" Did God change his mind? Who can know, for who can know the mind of God? One thing we do know is this: The sentence of death drove Hezekiah to throw himself upon the mercy and grace of God like he had never done before, and his life was changed because of it.

Perhaps you need to move the hand of God on your behalf today. If it was possible for Hezekiah, I believe it is possible for us as well. The changelessness of God is taught throughout the Scriptures; therefore, what he has done for others, he can do for us. The one thing that is certain is that we must first *act* before God will *react* on our behalf. Time and again, he told us in his Word that if we will call upon him with humble, clean, and obedient hearts, he will hear us; and if he hears us, we will have the petitions we desire of him.

Here is a man who defeated the very sentence of death. God in his mercy added many more years to his life. Would God do it again? Through the power of his grace and in accordance to his will, why not?

Can

Humans

Change

God's

Mind?

❖

127

*M*ay the words of my
mouth and the meditation of
my heart
be pleasing in your sight
O LORD, my Rock and my
Redeemer.

—Psalm 19:14

Chapter Ten

WHAT'S IN A WORD?

The Power of Self-Conversation

So often we are defeated, not by our circumstances, but by our attitudes. The things we believe about ourselves and the things we tell ourselves are powerful tools that Satan uses to keep us defeated and less than overcomers, robbing us of our joy. We have all heard stories of those who were told they were worthless and failures during their childhood and grew to be adults who believed what they were told. The sad thing is that most of the time, we do believe what we are told. And quite often, we believe what we tell ourselves even more.

Do you ever have your own private conversations? Do you talk to yourself? Certainly you do; we all do to one degree or another. The old adage is true: It is okay to argue with yourself—just be sure you never lose.

Have you ever seen a person sitting in a restaurant or driving down the road with his or her lips moving, having a self-conversation? All of us have chuckled at that at one time or another. But when we think about it, it is amazing how much of our lives are determined by words of self-conversation. Words can cheer us up, make us glad, change our outlook on life, and change our inlook concerning ourselves. The Bible says that the right words in the right place can be like "apples of gold in settings of silver" (Proverbs 25:11). Positive words can comfort, challenge, encourage, and restore. Negative words, on the other hand, can tear down, wreck, destroy, and demolish hearts and lives. The Bible says that "the tongue has the power of life and death" (Proverbs 18:21).

*T*HE POWER OF WORDS

David declared in Psalm 107:20: "He sent forth his word and healed them; he rescued them from the grave." The words that Jesus Christ spoke were always for the purpose of healing and restoration. The whole purpose of Christ's ministry was our deliverance. First and foremost, he delivered us from our sins, but he also delivered us from the effects of our sins through the power of his Word.

The Word of the Lord is of central importance. If you don't believe the Word of God, there will be no healing for you! The Bible is life and health. In fact, through all of Scripture we find that the words of God are consistently associated with life, health, and wholeness. John 6:63 says, "The Spirit gives life; the flesh counts for nothing. The words I have spoken to you are spirit and they are life." Solomon would even say that words "are life to those who find them and health to a man's whole body" (Proverbs 4:22).

Why are words so important? They are God's way of manipulating the visible universe. He created all things by his words. In Genesis 1 we see God's Spirit performing the words that he spoke. "And God said" is repeated over and over again. God's words, in the act of creation, were so powerful that to this day, people argue about the origin of the universe and even espouse that it began with some great explosion; that is the only thing they can imagine that would have so much power. But the writer of Hebrews tells us, "By faith we understand that the universe was formed at God's command, so that what is seen was not made out of what was visible" (Hebrews 11:3).

No words affect us more than the words we speak to ourselves. Whether we speak them audibly or not, what we say to ourselves is ultimately what we become. As the proverb puts it, "As he thinks in his heart, so is he" (Proverbs 23:7 NKJV).

Within the gospel, we see this clearly demonstrated in two instances when people spoke wrongly to themselves and two when people spoke rightly—and the results of the different kinds of self-talk.

THE NEGATIVE POWER OF WORDS

WORDS OF FOOLISHNESS

The first person we will look at is *a man of foolish words.* Luke 12:16–21 provides a parable from Jesus of a man who did not consider that God was in control of his life, but was overconsumed with the wealth that he had obtained. Consistently, Solomon tells us that seeking after possessions is foolish and that striving to obtain and keep those possessions is vanity. The man in Luke 12 is such a man. He was a farmer, and his land yielded bumper crops. We don't know much about his background or his family, but we do know him by the words he said to himself.

You would think that this man, looking at the great harvest he was given, would say, "Thank you, God, for all of your goodness. Thank you for the people who work for me; they've worked hard, and now I have more than I need. So I will share my wealth with them and with others in need and give you an offering of thanksgiving." This would be the biblical response, for Scripture tells us that "every good and perfect gift is from above, coming down from the Father of the heavenly lights" (James 1:17). We do not own anything, but God is the owner and keeper of all (see 1 Chronicles 29:11–12; Psalm 50:12). Unfortunately, this man did not respond biblically. For this man said to himself, "I will tear down my barns and build bigger ones, and there I will store all my grain and my goods. And I'll say to myself, 'You have plenty of good things laid up for many years. Take life easy; eat, drink and be merry'" (Luke 12:18–19).

This man was foolish for two reasons. First, he was foolish because he had no regard for God. We see no reference to God in his consideration. There was no thought of who had blessed his life or where the blessings had come from.

He thought only of himself. In fact, his conversation betrayed him when he said, "and there I will store up *my* grain and *my* goods."

Second, he was foolish because he did not regard others. This man was selfish. He did not see his possessions as a way that God could bless others through him. So often in our lives, we forget that all God gives us is to be used in service for him. The blessings God had given him were not for himself alone. God blessed him that he might bless others. His blessings had not been given to him to hoard or to keep for himself. This man's only thought was of himself, not of God or others. His words were the words of a fool.

This may sound harsh, but look at the next two verses of Luke 12. "But God said to him, 'You fool! This very night your soul will be demanded from you. Then who will get what you have prepared for yourself?' This is how it will be with anyone who stores up things for himself but is not rich toward God" (vv. 20–21). When we believe that we must acquire things or that possessions are more important than our relationship with God, we fall into the trap of materialism. Materialism can be a very powerful aspect of self-conversation. When we tell ourselves that we "need" this or that, we remove our focus from the provider of our needs, and we begin to focus on what we can accomplish.

WORDS OF PESSIMISM

Another pitfall that we must avoid is the *words of pessimism or negativity*. In Mark 2:1–12, Jesus is talking to a

What's in a Word?

❖

133

group of Pharisees who were afflicted with this form of self-conversation. Most of us know the story of the crippled man whose friends brought him to Jesus to be healed. Not being able to get into the house because it was too crowded, they took him up to the roof, tore back the shingles, and lowered him into the room. Jesus saw the crippled man and said unto him, "Son, your sins are forgiven" (v. 5). The Pharisees who were watching said within their hearts, "He's blaspheming! Who can forgive sins but God alone?" (v. 7). Right in the midst of the joy of the healed man, these negative, pessimistic souls were saying, "Who is this Jesus that he can forgive?"

So often in life, negativity creeps in. We have all known people who were pessimistic at heart. These people see the glass half empty instead of half full. Nothing can be more draining on one's life than to be pessimistic. In fact, in Matthew 5, Jesus spoke during his Sermon on the Mount about the secrets of joy. The opposite of joy is pessimism. Pessimists, by their own words, convince themselves that life is at best a mystery! Unfortunately, pessimism can be a very powerful factor in self-conversation. When people feed themselves negative conversation, they rob their lives of joy and excitement.

Pessimists insist on evidence and proof. They want nothing but the cold, hard facts. But a life that focuses on the cold, hard facts results in a cold, hard life. Not only is it impossible to please God without faith; it is impossible to live a happy, exciting life. Take away all of the faith from life, all of the adventure, and just require everything to be scientific facts, and see what that does to the exciting events of life. As it has been said, there are two different ways to look at life. We can look at life as an adventurist or as a rationalist. The adventurist would sing a song this way:

> Twinkle, twinkle little star,
>
> How I wonder what you are.
>
> Up above the world so high,
>
> Like a diamond in the sky.

But for the pessimist, or rationalist, the song would sound like this:

> Twinkle, twinkle little star,
>
> I know exactly what you are:
>
> An incandescent ball of gas
>
> Condensing to a solid mass.

Negative or pessimistic self-conversation are one of the enemy's strongest strategies for keeping us from being victorious in our Christian lives. We must be careful not to give Satan a foothold by continually doubting the power of God and believing that our situations are hopeless. In fact, Paul gives us the prescription for positive living in Philippians 4:13 when he said, "I can do everything through him who gives me strength." We are more than overcomers in this life, and God has not given us a spirit of fear but of power and of love and of a sound mind (see 2 Timothy 1:7).

Words of Victory

In contrast to the negative examples of self-talk, Jesus also gives us some positive examples to follow. In Matthew 9, Jesus tells us of a person who spoke to herself quite differently than the negative Pharisees and the foolish rich man. The Matthew passage tells us about a little lady whose life was in trouble. According to Scripture, "A woman who had been subject to bleeding for twelve years came up behind him and touched the edge of his cloak. She said to herself, 'If I only touch his cloak, I will be healed'" (vv. 20–21). Do not miss that Scripture says that when she heard of Jesus passing by, she said to herself words of great faith: "If I only touch his cloak, I will be healed."

This woman had been stricken with a terrible female disease. This disease would have made her an outcast in Jewish society because blood was considered unclean. It had likely cost her her marriage and the possibility of a family. She had spent all her money trying to get better, but she only grew worse (see Mark 5:26). Yet, when she considered the possibility of seeing Jesus and being in his presence, she risked rejection for the opportunity of healing.

She did not question the possibility that she might be healed. She did not doubt, even though she had had this problem for twelve years. What did she do? She stepped out on faith and did exactly what she told herself she would do. She touched his garment. Another account of this story tells us that when she touched him, Jesus sensed that power had left him. He turned around and began asking who had touched him. The disciples were puzzled by the question since many were gathered around him, pressing against him. Jesus was not asking who had simply touched him; he was asking who had been healed because of touching him. When the woman realized he was talking about her, she came before him, bowed at his feet, and worshiped him. She told him of her healing. Jesus then looked into her eyes and said, "Daughter, your faith has healed you. Go in peace" (Luke 8:48).

Now that is the kind of life worth living, not trapped in the mire of pessimism and fear but stepping out in a venture of faith! In our day, the security of materialism has caused many to forget the excitement of a life of faith. If it is not logical and reasonable to the average mind, it is not to be attempted. Many lose sight of the joy of faith. The joy of risking it all on God and his promises can be fulfilling. That's the kind of life that can make the Christian life exciting, daring, and meaningful.

You don't need to understand everything about God in order to believe in him and what he will do. The fact is, we understand very few things that we do in life.

In the book *The Nature of the Physical World*, Dr. Arthur Eddington wrote,

> I'm standing at the threshold of a door about to enter a room. That scientifically is a complicated business. First of all, I must shove against an atmosphere pressing with a

force of 14 lbs. on every square inch of my body. Then, I must step into the other room, which is traveling at 20 miles per second around the sun. I must do all this while hanging from a round planet, head outward, into space.[1]

Now, the next time you want to walk into a room, you can consider all of that, or you can simply walk in. Faith is simply walking into what God has promised. This little woman believed, touched, and was healed.

WORDS OF FORGIVENESS

Jesus provided another example of positive self-talk. This time, he told a parable of a young man who spoke to himself positive words of grace. This young fellow is found in Luke 15. This young man came to his father to seek his independence and asked his father for his share of the inheritance. Now speculate with me for a moment: Why would he do this? I envision that this young man told himself: "I'm a grownup now; I can take care of myself." Lloyd Ogilvie, in his book *Autobiography of God*, refers to this mind-set as the "stupidity of independence."[2]

So, this young man left his father's care to seek his own independence. We watch him squander his inheritance on partying and wild lifestyles. When he ran out of money, he had to make a living, but there was a famine in the land at the time. So he took the only work he could find—feeding pigs their slop. He even had to bed with them for shelter. This prodigal son had lost his money and friends and dignity. He had thought he knew more than his father. And with riotous living, he wasted all that he had been given. But in the midst of it all, he had a conversation with himself. In fact, the Bible says, "When he came to his senses, he said, 'How many of my father's hired men have food to spare, and here I am starving to death! I will set out and go back to my father and say to him: Father, I have sinned against heaven and against you. I am no longer worthy to be called your son; make me like one of your hired men'" (Luke 15:17–19).

Scripture then tells us that he got up, dusted himself off, and headed for home. But, while he was still some distance from home, his father saw him. The father must have been waiting, just hoping that his son would return. When the father saw his son, he jumped up and ran to him. He wrapped his arms around him and kissed him. As the boy was reciting his speech to his father, saying he was no longer worthy, his father stopped him in mid sentence. He cried to his servant, "Quick! Bring the best robe and put it on him. Put a ring on his finger and sandals on his feet. Bring the fattened calf and kill it. Let's have a feast and celebrate" (vv. 22–23). Can you imagine the mind of that boy? He probably could not believe the graciousness of his father and certainly was not prepared for it.

We sometimes have a hard time understanding the love and grace of God too. How could God forgive us? Love us? Restore us as he does? We tell ourselves that there is no way he would do that for us. But the fact of the matter is that he will and that he is looking for the moment to do so. The words of forgiveness are important for us to remember. First John 1:9 says that if we confess our sins, he is faithful and just to forgive our sins. God gives us a promise that he will forgive our sins if we come and ask him.

$\mathcal{T}$HE CHOICE IS YOURS

Self-conversation can be a powerful ally or enemy, depending on how we use it. Demosthenes once said, "Nothing is so easy as to deceive oneself; for what we wish, we readily believe." We must be careful in what we tell ourselves. In his book, *Telling Yourself the Truth*, William Backus says, "The words we tell ourselves are more important than we realize. If you tell yourself something enough times and in the right circumstances, you will believe those words whether true or not."[3]

So often in our lives, we defeat ourselves by negative self-conversation. Quite often, that comes from comparing ourselves to people or things that we should not. Backus asks,

> Are you comparing yourself and your life with someone else who seems better in some way, or are you looking at yourself in the light of God's word? D. L. Moody once said that the best way to show that a stick is crooked is not to argue about it or spend time denouncing it, but to lay a straight stick alongside it. The straight stick in the lives of Christians is the lovely and indestructible love of Christ.

When we realize what Christ has already done for us

and what he desires to do for us in the future, we have no reason to speak to ourselves the words of negativity. We can boldly proclaim to ourselves words of encouragement, faith, and forgiveness and remind ourselves that God loves us and he desires to make us whole.

When David was experiencing verbal abuse from the men in his armies, he got himself alone and "encouraged himself in the LORD" (1 Samuel 30:6 KJV). Do you need encouragement today? If so, it may come from friends and other acquaintances. But if not, why don't you just be your own best friend and "encourage yourself in the Lord"?

ℐELF-EXAMINATION

Ask yourself a few important questions concerning your own self-conversations.

- Do the words I speak into my life build up my faith, encourage my heart, and lift my spirit?
- Do the books I read and the television/radio/movies I expose myself to point my mind and heart toward the positive things of life?
- Do the people I call my friends help me grow positively in my walk of faith or do they influence my heart away from God?
- Are the thoughts of my mind and the meditations of my heart (self-conversations), acceptable to God who is my strength and my redeemer?

*P*eace I leave with you; my peace I give you. I do not give to you as the world gives. Do not let your hearts be troubled and do not be afraid.

—John 14:27

Chapter Eleven

IS THERE
NO PEACE?
Winning the Battle over Worry

Someone has said that worrying is like building bridges over rivers you will never cross. And I might add that building those useless bridges will drain from you time, effort, money, and emotions.

Now none of us wants to be "preached at" concerning worry. I think most folks know how useless it is without being told. But the problem is that knowing the foolishness of worry is one thing. Not worrying is another.

Most of us battle with feelings of concern, apprehension, fear, and even seasons of insecurity. Our hearts are in a state of unrest, and we have no peace. These are strong emotions that can trap us and keep us from experiencing the healing to which God calls us. One of the first things we must realize is that even though we see these emotions as

negative, they were created by God and do serve a vital purpose in our lives. They can protect us from harm, and they
caution us to plan for circumstances; but God did not design
them to control our lives. We were not created to be overwhelmed by concern, apprehension, fear, and insecurity.
When these emotions take control of our daily activities
and prevent healing, worry has an unhealthy hold on us. I
hope to provide some solutions to worry in this chapter.

*W*HAT ARE YOU WORRIED ABOUT?

Are you worried about something or someone today?
Rest assured, you are not the only one. There is much worry
in the world today. There are people who are worried about
terrorism, nuclear war, and the economy. There are others
who are worried about famine, disease, hunger, and starva-
tion. There are some who are worried about family, health,
work, and finances. Big or small, long- or short-term, we all
have things that we worry about—things that keep us up at
night, cause us to lose or gain weight, affect our moods, and
strain our relationships. Books are written about it, seminars
are conducted for it, and counselors charge hourly rates to
hear it. Our society is "A World of Worry."

Dr. Walter Cavert, a well-known Christian psycholo-
gist, surveyed a number of patients whose issues involved
worry. Here are some statistics of his discovery:

- 40 percent worried about things that never happened.

- 30 percent worried about things in the past that they could do nothing about.

- 12 percent worried about some imaginary illness they did not have.

- 10 percent worried about something that might happen to a loved one.

- Only 8 percent worried about something real.[1]

When we sum up the results, we can see that 92 percent of his patients had worries that were unfounded and unnecessary. These worries accomplished little more than to enslave these people to their fears. But whether these worries were actual or imagined, to the person who owned them, they were real.

It is not hard to see that worry affects a person's life—it warps the thinking; it squeezes all the joy out of life; it robs people of peace. The English word *worry* is derived from an Anglo-Saxon word that means "to strangle." And just like a weed strangles the life out of vegetation, so does worry strangle our souls.

DIVINE SOLUTIONS FOR DEFEATING WORRY

As damaging as worry can be, it should not be surprising, then, that Scripture gives us solutions for defeating it. Scripture tells the believer that there is a way out of worry, how to identify it, how to manage it, how to rid your life of it, and how to defeat it. We should, therefore, be encouraged that we have been given provisions for conquering worry in our lives. The word *worry* is used nineteen times in the New Testament. Sometimes it has a negative meaning and sometimes a positive meaning. It can mean both anxiety and care or concern. In this chapter, we will study how to identify and conquer the harmful side of worry. If you are trapped by worry, listen to what the Scriptures teach, and, more than just listen, apply these principles to your life today.

TAKE NO THOUGHT

In Matthew, Jesus was talking to the people gathered around him on a hillside near the Sea of Galilee. As he spoke to them about many topics that affected their lives, he raised the issue of worry. Many of them were worried about their wealth and provisions. He said to them:

> Therefore I say unto you, take no thought for your life, what ye shall eat, or what ye shall drink; nor yet for your body, what ye shall put on. Is not the life more than meat, and the body than raiment?
>
> Behold the fowls of the air: for they sow not, neither do they reap, nor gather into barns; yet your heavenly Father feedeth them. Are ye not much better than they?
>
> Which of you by taking thought can add one cubit unto his stature?
>
> And why take ye thought for raiment? Consider the lilies of the field, how they grow; they toil not, neither do they spin:
>
> And yet I say unto you, That even Solomon in all his glory was not arrayed like one of these.
>
> Wherefore, if God so clothe the grass of the field, which to day is, and to morrow is cast into the oven, shall he not much more clothe you, O ye of little faith?

Therefore take no thought, saying, What shall we eat? Or, What shall we drink? Or, Wherewithal shall we be clothed?

(For after all these things do the Gentiles seek:) for your heavenly Father knoweth that ye have need of all these things. (Matthew 6:25–32 KJV)

Notice how many times "take no thought" or "why take ye thought" occurs in these eight verses. How well Christ knew people then and knows us now! He knows how difficult it is for us to trust him for our provisions. But he wants us to know that he is capable and willing to take care of those things that we worry over. We worry about the future, about tomorrow, about the "what ifs." But what does it do but wreck our minds and torment our hearts? How can we change, prevent, or fix anything that happens tomorrow? Jesus tells us not to dwell on tomorrow—just trust him today, every day.

Take It One Day at a Time

The children of Israel were first-rate worriers. Their worry, like so much of ours today, grew out of a lack of trust in God. Although God had rescued them through mighty miracles and brought them out of bondage, at the first sign of difficulty, they were ready to bail out. In Exodus 14, as they approached the Red Sea, they noticed, probably heard, the chariots of Pharaoh's army coming after them. We read in verse 10 that they were terrified. They complained to Moses, saying it would have been better to remain slaves and die in bondage than to be facing this doom. They had so quickly forgotten how powerfully God had delivered them from bondage. How could they forget God's protection from the ten plagues that finally persuaded Pharaoh to release them?

But in spite of their ungrateful distrust, God patiently showed his provision by parting the sea, leading them to the other side, and annihilating the Egyptian army. God was teaching them to trust him one crisis at a time.

But soon, they were again consumed with worry about their circumstances. Within one month, they started worrying about the lack of food in the desert. In Exodus 16:3, they accused Moses of bringing them into the desert to starve them to death. But once again, God, being faithful, provided them with the ultimate food provision. But with the provision came a lesson in daily trust. Every morning, manna was provided for that day and that day only. If they tried to plan ahead for tomorrow and gather extra manna, the leftover manna rotted. Only on the Sabbath were they allowed to store up food for an extra day. Every meal was dependent on their trust in him to provide for them one day at a time—not worrying about tomorrow's fare. How often do we behave like the Israelites and try to storehouse God's provisions in fear that he won't do the same tomorrow?

Taking it one day at a time means being in daily contact with our heavenly Father. I'm reminded of the story of a king who gave his son part of his inheritance on a certain day each year. Each year, when the day arrived for him to receive his money, the son made the annual visit to the palace of his father. But at no other time of the year would he come. One day the king sent word to his son that he was no longer going to give out the inheritance only once a year; it would now be divided into daily portions to be given out each day. Why? Because the king knew that under this new arrangement, he would have the joy of seeing his son every day.

Our heavenly Father wants us to be in daily contact with him as well. This daily contact is one sure way to help us take it one day at a time.

STAY FOCUSED

Not only should we learn to take one day at a time, but we should also learn to do one thing at a time. Rather than cluttering your mind with worry of things that will happen tomorrow, just do your best, with God's help, with the things that are before you today. How often do we get ourselves into trouble by worrying about forty things at once and doing every one of them with half an effort? Paul said, "One thing I do" (Philippians 3:13). He meant that he had singleness of purpose. He knew what really mattered: God's plan for his life. Everything else was secondary.

I remember moving into the dormitories at boarding school. I soon became wrapped up in all of the extracurricular activities. I had my favorite things to do: basketball, listening to the radio, and playing Monopoly. In the evenings, I would sit down to study and turn on the radio. Soon, I would need a break from study and get out the Monopoly board. In a short time, I would be so wrapped up in listening to the music and radio shows and playing a game that my studies did not have my undivided attention. My mind was worried and distracted with other things. Then, at test time, I could never understand why my grades were not as good as they should have been.

In that same way, we clutter our minds with worry about extracurricular activities that distract from our primary purpose. We get so caught up in worrying about the car needing a tune-up, school starting in a month, or tax time, that we lose sight of what God wants us to do today. I remember an old saying,

> Life is hard, yard by yard.
> Inch by inch, it's a cinch.

Give God the Best of Your Time

I'm sure you're saying by now, "Easier said than done." And I understand. If the Israelites had problems with letting go of worry, how are we any better? But there is a guaranteed way to be worry free more often. And that is by giving God the best of our time. What are our priorities? Where do we put God in our day? Matthew 6:33 says, "Seek first his kingdom and his righteousness." Is this a regular practice in your day? It is no wonder that people worry and have anxiety about their lives when they put God on the back burner.

The definition of anxiety in the believer is "the distance between God and you." When we distance ourselves from God by not spending time with him, worry and anxiety are inevitable. We have less assurance that God is taking care of things when we are not taking care of our relationship with him. But when we are close to God, we have a better understanding and confidence that God has things under control. Our relationship with him is directly proportional to our level of worry over things in our lives.

We cannot grow close to him and maintain that relationship unless we give him the best of our time.

When two people fall in love, it is impossible to separate them. They are either together, on the phone wishing they were together, or daydreaming about the next time they will be together. When the couple schedules time together, one does not say to the other, "If it's convenient, I'll see if I can work you into my schedule for a date Saturday night." Instead, one would say, "What time will you be ready?" or "What time will you pick me up?" Why? They love each other and want to give each other the best of their time. And anytime is the best time to give each other. If we love God, we'll give him the best of our time. If we give him the best of our time, we will find ourselves without time to worry.

If we are managing our time well enough to give God the best of it, then it becomes easy to trust God with the rest of it. Matthew 6:30 says, "If that is how God clothes the grass of the field, which is here today and tomorrow is thrown into the fire, will he not much more clothe you?" God knows what occupies your time. He knows what needs to be done with your time. He also knows how much of your time you spend worrying. And Jesus assures us that he is capable of taking care of it all. Verse 32 says, "Your heavenly Father knows that you need them."

Put Your Burdens Down

How many burdens and worries are you carrying daily? How much do you try to do on your own? The apostle Peter meant it when he said, "Cast all your anxiety on him because he cares for you" (1 Peter 5:7). Rest in this promise and know that there is nothing that he is not willing and not wanting to handle for his children. But he will not storm through your life taking charge. He patiently waits for you to look to

him and admit that you cannot handle it alone.

We can walk through life like the hitchhiker who was standing alongside the road, waiting for help, and carrying a heavy backpack filled with his belongings. This hitchhiker didn't know from where his help would come; he just knew that he needed it. After a time, a farmer stopped to help and let him ride in the bed of his truck. The farmer began driving down the road, taking him as far as he could. At one point, the farmer looked back at the man and noticed that he was still wearing his backpack. He laughed to himself and shouted through the window, "Man, I'm carrying you, so why are you still carrying your burden?"

We do the same thing. We travel through life, carrying our needs. We finally decide that we need help, and we call out to God. But when God sends the help, we don't know how to put down our burden. We don't know how to stop carrying the baggage. We have carried it for so long. We have it properly packed. No one else can carry it long enough to make a difference anyway, we think. So we continue to hold on to it. We forget that God is capable, that he is willing, and that he wants so much for us to lean on him and put down our burdens.

PRAY

Philippians 4:6–9 teaches us how to win over worry through prayer. Paul gives us a formula for communicating our needs and worries to the Lord and teaches us how to overcome anxiety. He gives us a "how-to," practical lesson in powerful prayer. "Do not be anxious about anything, but in everything, by prayer and petition, with thanksgiving, present your requests to God. And the peace of God, which transcends all understanding, will guard your hearts and your minds in Christ Jesus." The word *anxious* is the same Greek word as *worry*. The Bible simply proclaims to us that we are not to be anxious or worried about anything; instead, we are to bring our worries to God in prayer. Not only does Scripture stress prayer to defeat worry; it provides the steps to follow.

❖

153

Step #1: Praise

The first step is *praise*. The word *prayer* in verse 6 means "adoration" and "praise." It is not referring to the generic means of communicating to God but to a specific kind of communication—*praise*.

Paul, the writer of this book, was well acquainted with times of worry in his ministry. One such time was when he and Silas were locked in a jail at Philippi (see Acts 16). They had been preaching in the town, and some were being converted. But their words angered the idol merchants— who made quite a good living selling idols of popular gods in the marketplace. The merchants began to fear that this new message would affect their businesses. They became so enraged that they gathered a mob and hunted down Paul and Silas. The mob then brought them before the magistrates, who ordered that they be stripped and severely beaten and thrown into the deepest part of the prison and kept under heavy guard.

When Paul and Silas were put into the jail, Acts 16 tells us that they began singing praises to God and glorifying him in the midst of their distress. Their tribulation and persecution did not discourage them from giving adoration and praise to God. In the middle of the night, God responded to their prayers and intervened on their behalf. He caused a great earthquake, so that the walls of the prison shook. Immediately, all of the doors flew open, and the shackles fell off their wrists.

The jailer had fallen asleep during the night and was awakened by the quake. When he noticed the doors wide open, his first thought was that the prisoners had escaped. It was his responsibility to keep the prison secure, and punishment for letting the prisoners escape would probably have been death by execution. So he decided to take his own life by his sword rather than be tortured by his superiors. As he reached for his sword, Paul cried out and told him not to harm himself because all of the prisoners were still inside. The jailer was so relieved and impacted by their testimony that he fell at their feet and asked how he could be saved.

Paul had certainly learned from experience to rely on prayer—and specifically praise—to overcome his worry. Do not miss the fact that our text was originally written to the very people of this city. Most likely, one of the people reading the letter of Philippians was the very jailer who guarded them in that prison. He was no doubt acquainted with worry on that night and realized that praising God was a powerful weapon of healing over the situations that capture our minds.

Praise and adoration do two things for us when we incorporate them into prayer. First, praise brings our minds into focus on God and off of our problems. It is impossible to be in an attitude of praise and still dwell on our problems. David's psalms are evidence of that. We see several psalms that were written during times of persecution or trial. But in the course of a psalm, as he begins praising God, he focuses on his problems less and less. Quite often, his psalms end without reference to the problem that caused him to begin writing in the first place. Scripture says that God inhabits the praise of his people (see Psalm 22:3). Whenever God is praised, he is present.

Second, adoration brings us into his presence. When we express our adoration of him and focus on his attributes, we come face to face with him and his glory. What easier way to forget about our worries than to stand in the presence of Almighty God and proclaim our adoration of him!

Step #2: Supplication

Returning to the Philippians passage, Paul also lists *supplication* as a means of prayer. Supplication simply means telling God your need. Throughout this chapter, I have been showing how we must communicate our needs to God. Paul told us this almost two thousand years ago. We must take the time to share our needs with him. This is done in supplication during our prayer. We must specifically and clearly present our needs and our worries to the Father. He knows our needs before we ask them, but he desires for us to be in relationship with him. The way we do that is to talk to him and share our life events with him on a regular basis.

Step #3: Thanksgiving

The third aspect of our prayer is *thanksgiving*. Paul says, "in everything give thanks" (1 Thessalonians 5:18 NKJV). This is more than the child's prayer of "God is great, God is good, let us thank him for our food." While that is basic, we are challenged to enter into a deeper form of thanksgiving—a thanksgiving that expresses the faith that God will do what you have asked and that demonstrates the confidence that God is intervening on our behalf. Our thanksgiving is our statement of faith that God is going to meet our needs. It's saying, "Father, I praise you. Here is my petition. I thank you now for handling this situation." We give thanks because we know—not that God *will* help us, but that God *has been* helping us and will continue to do so.

Someone once categorized faith in these three levels:

1. Little faith says, "God, I know you can."
2. Great faith says, "God, I believe that you will."
3. Perfect faith says, "Thank you, Lord, it's already done."

THINK POSITIVELY

Scripture also tells us that we can overcome worry by *thinking in a positive way*. Philippians 4:8 says, "Finally brothers, whatever is true, whatever is noble, whatever is right, whatever is pure, whatever is lovely, whatever is admirable—if anything is excellent or praiseworthy—*think* about such things" (emphasis added). As we studied in the last chapter, Scripture repeatedly tells us to control our thoughts. Proverbs 23:7 says, "As he *thinks* in his heart, so is he" (NKJV, emphasis added). Paul says, "Let this *mind* be in you, which was also in Christ Jesus" (Philippians 2:5 KJV, emphasis added).

We are responsible for maintaining our thought life in a godly way. When Satan tempts us to worry and have fear, we begin to dwell on the negative. If we continue down a path of worry, we can become bitter or depressed and lose control over our lives.

But God is our Healer, and he wants us to dwell on the positive. What positive things does God want us to think on? Paul tells us in the Philippians 4 passage above. First, he wants us to think on things that are *true*. Simply, these are the thoughts that are not lies. So many times, we worry about things that just aren't true. We can become consumed by lies we have heard from others or have told ourselves. Then, he tells us to think on things that are *noble* and *right*. These thoughts focus on the good things of life and not the troubles of others. It means to refrain from gossip and slander and not to fill the mind with television or music or conversation that is harmful or hurtful. Finally, he tells us to think on things that are *pure* and *lovely* and *admirable*. These are the great things, the lasting things. These are the thoughts of purity and beauty, the ones that are clean and wholesome. When we think on those things we become living vessels of faith and are capable of helping others find healing from this same spiritual sickness.

Accept God's Peace

The next step in Paul's formula is to *accept God's peace in a practical way*. After outlining the different kinds of prayer we are to bring to God, Paul says, "And the peace of God, which transcends all understanding, will guard your hearts and your minds in Christ Jesus" (Philippians 4:7). Then in verse 8, after telling us to think on positive things, Paul once again ties in the concept of *peace*—but not until he exhorts us to live out in a practical way what we've learned from him: "Whatever you have learned or received or heard from me, or seen in me—put into practice. And the God of peace will be with you" (v. 9). Paul wants us to understand that God's peace *can* be ours. And isn't peace what we long for most when we are overwhelmed with worry? Paul uses words like *learn, receive, hear,* and *see* to express his desire that we understand that God is in control and that he is working in our lives today. We need to understand that the Creator, the God of the universe, allowed his Son to die for our sins to fulfill a plan. He is not going to let that plan fail now! He did not create us to be defeated but assures us victory in our lives. So many people have a tendency to spiritualize the Bible that they forget to understand the practical peace it offers. The Bible was written to be a manual, describing how God loves and cares for his children —and this understanding dispels worry and fills us with *peace.*

LIVE PRODUCTIVELY

The last step to follow for victory over worry is to *live in a productive way.* The end of verse 9 reads, "Whatever you have learned...put into practice." We are to keep ourselves busy doing the things that we have learned in God's Word to do. The most discouraging, lonely thing in the world is to have nothing to do. Most people who have nothing to do spend most of their time in worry. An old saying holds an important truth for us: An idle mind is the devil's workshop. Satan knows how to get a nonproductive Christian to start concentrating on worrisome things. Paul says in essence, "Get busy…do the things you have learned to do."

❖

God has a purpose for your life. And at any stage of your life, he is willing to heal you of sickness. He understands that we encounter this temptation and fall into the sin of worry. But he is faithful and waiting for us to call upon him for healing. Only after we have done that can we experience the healing needed in our lives. And only after we have experienced healing, can we lead productive lives in a right relationship with him. Let your healing begin, and let it begin today.

❖

When Jesus had again crossed over by boat to the other side of the lake, a large crowd gathered around him while he was by the lake. Then one of the synagogue rulers, named Jairus, came there. Seeing Jesus, he fell at his feet and pleaded earnestly with him, "My little daughter is dying. Please come and put your hands on her so that she will be healed and live."

—*Mark 5:21–23*

Chapter Twelve

HOW CAN I RECEIVE THE HEALING TOUCH OF JESUS?

Coming to the Feet of Jesus

Why does the healing process sometimes take so much effort on our part? Of course, in reality, none of the effort comes from us; it all comes from God. But, nonetheless, the process of seeking healing is not always easy. In this chapter, we'll examine three of the healing miracles of Jesus to learn what obstacles the healed ones had to overcome, and three qualities that brought them into contact with the healing touch of Jesus.

THREE STORIES OF PEOPLE WHO WERE TOUCHED BY JESUS' HEALING HAND

It is impossible to know how many miracles Jesus actually performed while on this earth. Matthew recorded that

"Jesus went throughout Galilee…healing every disease and sickness among the people…. All who were ill…demon-possessed…having seizures, and…paralyzed,…he healed" (Matthew 4:23–24). Mark recorded that "the people brought to Jesus all the sick and demon-possessed.…and Jesus healed many" (Mark 1:32–34) and "all who touched him were healed" (Mark 6:56). The writers of the Gospels record twenty-seven healing miracles of Jesus Christ. (For a complete list of the miracles recorded in the Gospels, see the appendix. We will not examine all twenty-seven miracles in this chapter, but we will look at three to learn three qualities we can grow in our lives as we seek his healing touch.

Before we examine these three qualities, let's set the stage by reviewing the three miracles.

Jairus's Daughter Raised

The story of Jairus's daughter is actually intertwined with our second healing; in fact, the second miracle interrupted the first. Both are told in three of the Gospels (see Matthew 9:18–26; Mark 5:22–43; Luke 8:41–56) and began as Jesus returned from a boat excursion that had taken him from the Gadarenes, where he cast a legion of demons from a wild man, to Capernaum, on the western side of the Sea of Galilee. While crossing the sea, a great storm had erupted, which Jesus stilled with a mere word. When Jesus and his disciples landed on shore, they were met by a large crowd (see Luke 8:40; Mark 5:21). It is likely that other boats were on the sea when Jesus calmed the storm and had spread the word of the miracle, and some may have heard reports of the deliverance of the demoniac. The crowds were no doubt expectant and exuberant as Jesus stepped ashore.

Jairus, one of the synagogue rulers, was among the enthusiastic crowd. He must have felt an extreme sense of urgency as he approached Jesus with his request: "My little daughter is dying. Please come and put your hands on her so that she will be healed and live" (Mark 5:23). Mark and Luke depict Jairus as describing his daughter's condition as critical; she was dying. Matthew's much more direct account suggests that she had already died. As precious time lapsed, it is not difficult to imagine that Jairus may have suspected that the worst had already happened. Nevertheless, even if she had died, Jairus believed that Jesus' touch could heal her (see Matthew 9:18–19). Jesus consented, and they set out toward Jairus's house. But an interruption that would steal valuable time was in the making. A woman was diligently working her way through the crowd, making her way to Jesus.

After Jesus dealt with the woman in his own special way (we'll examine that later), a servant from the house of Jairus approached and informed the Healer and the seeker that the child was already dead. They had delayed too long. He advised that there was no need to come.

But the advice of the messenger was wrong, and Jesus quickly countered it with these words to Jairus: "Don't be afraid; just believe, and she will be healed" (Luke 8:50).

How Can I

Receive the

Healing

Touch of

Jesus?

❖

165

When Jesus arrived at the house of Jairus, he did not let any go in with him except three of his closest disciples. A large crowd had already gathered to mourn the child's death, and they were making quite a commotion. Jesus told them to be quiet (see Mark 5:39), and he further told them that the girl was not dead, but asleep. Mourning turned to scornful laughter. They knew that she was dead!

Both Matthew and Mark tell us that these scorners and mourners were put outside the house before Jesus dealt with the death of the daughter (see Matthew 9:23–25; Mark 5:40). Luke does not bother with this detail. He simply tells us that Jesus took the child by the hand and commanded her to arise (see Luke 8:54). Immediately her spirit returned, and she arose. She stood up and walked around. Her parents were both astonished and delighted. Jesus then gave two perplexing commands.

The first was that they give the girl something to eat. One would think that if Jesus could raise this girl from the dead, he could also have done so with a full stomach. And so he could have. I believe that there is a very important principle suggested here: God does not do for people what they can do for themselves. God has come in the person of Christ to help those who cannot help themselves. Jairus could not heal his sick daughter or raise her when she died. Jesus could, and he did. But Jairus and his wife could feed the child, and so Jesus did not do so, miraculously. Miracles are not performed where normal human effort is sufficient.

Our Lord's second command is also of interest, but for a

different reason. He commanded the parents not to tell anyone what had happened (see Luke 8:56). Was Jesus trying to keep this miracle a secret? There were many waiting outside to see what would happen. The girl would sooner or later appear alive. In fact, everyone did learn that she had been raised. Matthew reports, "News of this spread through all that region" (Matthew 9:26). Jesus was not trying to prevent the impossible here. Instead, he was sternly insisting that those who had scoffed would be deprived not only of witnessing this miracle, but also of hearing a firsthand testimony of what had happened.

Think of the frustration and irritation of those who had laughed at Jesus, who upon seeing the girl alive, could not hear from the parents what had happened inside. "Tell us what happened," they must have inquired, only to be told, "I'm sorry, Jesus told us very emphatically not to tell you." Those who disbelieve not only fail to receive God's blessings; they are not even able to witness them.

The Woman with the Flow of Blood

The woman in this story, whose name is never given, had suffered from a hemorrhage for twelve years. Her ailment was probably female in nature.

This woman slipped up behind Jesus—not wanting to draw attention to herself—reached out her hand, and secretly touched Jesus' garment. At the moment of contact with his garment, the woman was instantly healed of her twelve-year ailment. Jesus, knowing that healing power had left him, stopped, not willing to go on until the person who had touched him was known. All of this took time, precious time, which seemed to endanger the daughter of Jairus. We are not told of Jairus's response, but Luke informs us that the disciples (Peter in particular) were disturbed by Jesus' actions.

TWO BLIND MEN

❖

The third miracle we'll look at is the healing of two blind men. This story is recounted only by Matthew. The Gospels record several other stories of blind being people healed (see Matthew 12:22, 20:30, 21:14; Mark 8:22–26; John 9), but none seem to parallel this story.

After Jesus left Jairus's house, two blind men heard that Jesus was passing by, and they called out to him—but Jesus didn't stop; he went into a house. It is assumed that at least Peter, James, and John were with him, so perhaps they went into one of their houses in Capernaum, since Jesus did not have his own house (see Matthew 8:20).

> As Jesus went on from there, two blind men followed him, calling out, "Have mercy on us, Son of David!"
> When he had gone indoors, the blind men came to him, and he asked them, "Do you believe that I am able to do this?"
> "Yes, Lord," they replied.
> Then he touched their eyes and said, "According to your faith will it be done to you"; and their sight was restored. (Matthew 9:27–30)

In the Near East, eye diseases were as repulsive as leprosy. So touching them had special significance. Notice that

Jesus didn't just talk to them; he actually touched them at the point of their need.

The fact that the men identified him as the "Son of David" also had special significance. This is the first time Jesus was addressed as such; this was a title that referred to his Messiahship, and it shows that the blind men recognized Jesus as the Messiah.

It is interesting to note that all three of these healings included some sort of obstacle: The healing of Jairus's daughter was delayed, and because of the delay, she died before Jesus arrived. The woman who approached Jesus, secretly, from behind, had to press her way through a pushy crowd. The two blind men who pursued Jesus were first ignored by him before he finally healed them.

Why is healing sometimes difficult for us to obtain? What qualities can we learn from these three healings that we can develop in our own lives as we seek the healing touch of Jesus?

*W*HAT CAN I BRING TO THE FEET OF JESUS?

CONTINUED FAITH WHEN HEALING IS DELAYED

For a short time in our story, it appeared that the interaction with the woman in the crowd had cost the life of Jairus's daughter. The question begs to be asked: Why would Jesus take the time to identify the person who touched him when doing so could endanger the life of a little girl who was virtually at death's door?

And on top of that, the woman didn't even want to be identified. She'd hoped that after touching Jesus, he and the crowd would continue on, leaving her alone, unnoticed, and able to return to her home and a normal life. But Jesus would not have it this way. Astounding the disciples and the rest of the crowd, Jesus stopped and inquired as to who had touched him.

Seeking the identity of one particular person in such a teeming crowd was seemingly an impossible task. More than that, it seemed to be a fruitless task. What difference did it make anyway?

Initially, no one admitted touching Jesus. Everyone—Luke informs us—denied touching him. Peter spoke for the others when he said, "Master, the people are crowding and pressing against you" (Luke 8:45). There seemed to be a stalemate. But Jesus would not let the matter drop, even though the disciples protested.

Finally, the woman recognized that she must confess. Fearfully, she came to Jesus and fell at his feet. Before the crowd, she bore witness as to why she had touched him, and how he had healed her (see v. 47). Jesus had very few words to say to the woman, but they were very important words: "Daughter, your faith has healed you. Go in peace" (v. 48).

For this, Jesus had stopped, refusing to go on to the house of Jairus, until he could say those potent words to this hurting woman. Why were the words of the woman and the words of Jesus so important? Why would Jesus delay that urgent journey to the house of Jairus, only to learn who had touched him, even if it had produced a healing? In actuality, God orchestrated this delay for the benefit of all involved, including Jairus and his daughter. He delayed for several reasons.

Jesus Wanted Her to Face Her Savior

Jesus would not allow the woman to remain anonymous. Note the position of the woman, before and after she identified herself to Jesus. Before, she was behind Jesus, out of his sight (or so she thought). After he confronted her, she was at his feet, just as Jairus had been. The woman had come to Jesus in secret, from behind, because she felt unworthy to approach him directly. Jesus would not allow this thinking to stand. He would not be content until she, just like Jairus, the ruler of the synagogue, was before him, looking into his face. This is where people of faith belong: before him, at his feet. Only those who are unbelievers will have God's back turned to them.

Jesus Wanted the True Cause of Her Healing Known

Second, Jesus would have no misunderstanding as to the real cause of the woman's healing. If Jesus had not identified faith as the real source of the woman's healing, some may have attributed it to other causes, maybe even to magic rather than faith. Jesus identified *faith* as the real cause of the miracle. She believed, as the other Gospels record, that if she were to touch Jesus she would be healed. She not only believed this in her head, she acted on it in her heart. As we have seen, touching Jesus was not an easy thing to do, but she did it. From one point of view, it was Jesus' power that healed her; but from another (the point of view Jesus does not wish to be overlooked), it was the woman's faith that brought her healing. Jesus thought this concept important enough to delay the healing of Jairus's daughter.

Jesus Did Not Want the Woman to Experience False Guilt

❖

172

If Jesus had not made the woman face him, she may have gone home healed, but feeling guilty. After all, in some sense, she had stolen the healing from Jesus. She had taken it without permission, and, she may have thought, without his knowledge. Jesus' words, "Go in peace," suggest that she could go home without any misgivings, without any guilt. She had not "stolen" a healing from Jesus; he had given it to her, as a gift of grace. Grace has no guilt, and Jesus would have her know that she has been endowed not only with divine power, but also with divine grace.

Jesus Did Not Want Her Faith to Remain Anonymous

Finally, Jesus delayed the healing of Jairus's daughter to ensure that the woman's faith not remain anonymous. It is not the miracle that Jesus wanted to make public but rather the woman's faith. Jairus's faith was very evident as he fell before the Lord Jesus and begged him to come to his house. But the woman had tried to remain anonymous as she reached out to Jesus in faith, she had done so anonymously. Jesus did not allow her faith to remain unknown.

Faith in Christ must be publicly professed. "If you confess with your mouth, 'Jesus is Lord,' and believe in your heart that God raised him from the dead, you will be saved. For it is with your heart that you believe and are justified, and it is with your mouth that you confess and are saved. As the Scripture says, 'Anyone who trusts in him will never be put to shame' " (Romans 10:9–11). Faith is not intended to be a private matter, as so many seem to think. How often have I heard people decline to discuss their spiritual condition, justifying themselves with the statement, "Well, my faith is a very personal thing." Faith in Christ is not only personal.

How Can I

Receive the

Healing

Touch of

Jesus?

❖

173

Jesus acknowledged that it was the woman's faith that healed her, but he also insisted that she confess her faith before men. This was so important that our Lord refused to go on without her confession of faith.

Divine Delays May Bring Extra Blessings

Sometimes, delays result in greater blessings. The delay that we find in our text was a divine delay; it was one that resulted from our Lord's decision and actions. If our Lord had not stopped and insisted on knowing who touched him, his arrival at Jairus's home would not have been delayed at all. It was not the woman's actions that slowed Jesus down, but our Lord's actions. She did not create the delay, Jesus did. It was a divine delay.

❖

If the cause of the delay was divine, the effect of the delay was a blessing. The delay focused attention on her faith and on her healing. It showed that she had equal access to the Savior and that Jesus delighted in her healing.

But the delay was also a blessing to Jairus. Just as our Lord's delay in going to Lazarus resulted in a raising from the dead, rather than a "mere" healing, so our Lord's delay in arriving at the home of Jairus resulted in a greater miracle: a raising from the dead, rather than a healing. This greater healing required greater faith from Jairus, and it brought greater glory to our Lord. It also revealed the lack of faith on the part of those who came to report the girl's death and on the part of the mourners who had begun to weep and wail over her death.

Jesus could easily have prevented the girl from dying, whether present or absent (see Luke 7:2–10), but he chose to overcome death instead. The divine delay was, then, for the good of all involved.

Each of us has experienced God's delays too. He has, for example, delayed his coming. He could have already come, but out of his long-suffering, he has delayed, for his coming will bring judgment on all unbelievers. Whatever it is that we have asked God to do now, whatever it is that has been delayed in our lives, if God has promised to do it, it will be done. As you wait on him, may your faith abound. The greater the delay, the greater our delight when God proves himself faithful.

The woman's effort to reach out and touch Jesus' garment may seem an insignificant gesture, but for this woman, it was a great accomplishment that deserves our attention. We can learn from her persistence not to be deterred by obstacles that seem to stand between us and the healing we desire. Three incredible obstacles could have prevented her faith-filled reach.

Ceremonial Uncleanness

First, this woman had to overcome the obstacle of her ceremonial uncleanness, as defined by the Old Testament Law. The Book of Leviticus clearly identifies this woman's condition as one that made her unclean and should, therefore, have restricted her to her own home. Under Old Testament Law, when a woman had her regular flow of blood—her monthly period—she was considered impure for seven days, and anyone who touched her was unclean till evening. When a woman had a discharge of blood for many days at a time other than her monthly period or had a discharge that continued beyond her period, she was considered unclean as long as she had the discharge. Any bed she lay on while her discharge continued was unclean, and anything she sat on was unclean. Whoever touched her was unclean and must wash his or her clothes and bathe with water and would be unclean till evening (see Leviticus 15:19, 25–27).

How Can I

Receive the

Healing

Touch of

Jesus?

175

Her unclean state would have made her repulsive to the crowd she passed through on her way to Jesus. But her faith was stronger than her fear of rejection, and she made her way toward the One she believed could save her.

The Difficulty of the Crowd

In order to get to Jesus, this woman had to work her way through a large crowd. Luke tells us that there was a large crowd and that they were pressing hard upon our Lord. As Jesus was making his way to Jairus's house, the crowds almost crushed him (see Luke 8:42). We must say, then, that getting to Jesus would have been no easy task for anyone. The crowd may have parted to allow Jairus, a synagogue ruler, access to the Savior; but they would not have done so for anyone of a lesser status—especially an *unclean woman*. Nevertheless, this determined woman fought her way through that churning crowd.

Weakened Physical Condition

Not only did this woman have a large crowd to contend with, she was also in a weakened physical condition. It would have been difficult enough for a woman in top physical condition to get through the crowd to Jesus, but this woman suffered from a prolonged illness, one which had gotten progressively worse (see Mark 5:26), and thus her condition was very poor. It may have been a major undertaking for her to get up out of bed, let alone fight her way through a crowd.

Finally, the woman had to reach Jesus by forcing her way through an aggressive and crushing mob, in a way that did not draw attention to herself. It is especially clear in Luke's account that the woman desired to remain a mystery: "Then the woman, seeing that she could not go unnoticed, came trembling and fell at his feet" (Luke 8:47). It is not hard to see why the woman would have wanted to remain unnoticed: She was a woman; she was a woman with a condition that made her unclean; she was a woman with a female problem that she would not care to proclaim before a large crowd. Her goal was to force her way through the crowd without being noticed. And the amazing thing is that she did so.

A SPECIAL KIND OF "HOPELESS FAITH"

The three miracles that we have witnessed through the Gospels had a great impact on those who experienced them, even if their meaning and message was not perceived by the crowds. But these miracles were also meant for the benefit of us today. In the characters of these three stories we see a kind of "hopeless faith." For we see that when all earthly hope is gone, true faith can finally kick in.

Hope Is the Product of Faith

The three healings we've looked at demonstrate that hope is the product of faith, and not the other way around: Faith is not the product of hope. The woman who sneaked up behind Jesus came to him after she'd exhausted all other efforts, after she'd seen all the doctors and spent all her money. She'd been bleeding for twelve years; she had no remaining options. All human hope was gone. Faith was not the result of hope (human hope) but the response to the absence of it.

The same can be said for Jairus. The messengers who came to report the girl's death seemed to believe that there was hope of the girl's healing as long as she was alive. But once she died, they saw no hope, and thus they counseled Jairus not to bother the Teacher any longer.

The mourners gathered inside Jairus's house felt the same way. When Jesus said the girl was asleep rather than dead, they laughed in unbelief. They saw no hope. The funeral might just as well go on. But Jairus's words, as recorded in Matthew, reinforced by our Lord's encouragement, indicate that faith has hope when all human hope is gone.

Even the two blind men were without human hope. Their "hopeless" faith drew them to their only true hope— the Messiah, the Son of David.

Faith That Still Has Human Options Is Meager Faith

Biblical faith has God as its object when all other options are gone. One reason that Jesus spent so much time among the helpless and the hopeless was because they were ripe for faith. They knew better than to put their trust in mere mortals or human wisdom. Many people reject God because they have too many other things in which to trust. When God pulls the rug out from under us, when he removes all other options, then we must trust in him and him alone. May we develop the quality of "hopeless faith" as we come to Jesus Christ, and to him alone.

How Can I

Receive the

Healing

Touch of

Jesus?

❖

179

FORTITUDE WHEN YOUR FAITH IS TESTED

Why did Jesus initially pass by the two blind men who called out for his help? Did he intend to help them all along? Was he testing their persistence, their faith? We don't know for sure, but we do know that there are occasions in all of our lives when our faith is tested, when we are asked to reach a little further, to believe a little deeper.

The two blind men already believed that Jesus was merciful—thus their appeal, "Have mercy on us" (Matthew 9:27)—and they knew that he was the Messiah, for they called him the Son of David. But Jesus wanted to know if they believed in *him*, if they believed that he could heal them. Their response was an immediate, "Yes, Lord!" This is the response he wants from us as well.

Though these men were blind, they had more spiritual sight than all the nation's leaders. They had not seen any miracles, while the nation had witnessed at least seventeen by now and still missed the point. Many of the Jews would even accuse Jesus of performing the miracles by Satan's power.

We also see faith tested in the lives of the others we've studied. Jairus's faith was tested when he was required to wait while Jesus interacted with the woman at his feet, and the woman was required to cast aside her fear of rejection and proclaim her faith before an unfriendly crowd.

Like these two blind men, whatever physical handicaps you may have, they do not prevent you from gaining deep, spiritual insight. And like the woman who tried to remain anonymous, you, too, can overcome your fears and fall at the feet of Jesus. Like Jairus, you can learn to trust when all earthly hope is gone. And just as Jesus touched their lives and offered them healing, he touches you where you hurt and offers hope.

❖

ONLY GOD
CAN HEAL

As we have seen, Jesus' healing touch was displayed frequently and powerfully in his miracles. Each time he reached out to someone in physical or emotional distress, he met the needs of their total being. For Jesus, healing involved helping the total person. He was just as concerned about their spiritual lives as he was about their physical needs.

Experiencing the healing touch of Jesus today can be as real as when he walked the shores of Galilee twenty centuries ago. Today, the same living Savior reaches out to touch us and transform our lives. His grace is still sufficient, and his power is still great enough to lift us up with hope.

His heart has not changed. His love is not diminished. He still cares about our physical, emotional, and spiritual hurts. He stands ready to meet each need we have, when we learn to reach out to him through faith.

Two things are especially clear when we look at the biblical teaching of healing: (1) only God can heal, and (2) faith in God is vital to our healing.

$\mathcal{W}$E CANNOT HEAL OURSELVES

The God who made us is the only one who can heal us. He may empower some people with a powerful faith in our behalf, but only God can do the healing.

Prayer is one of the key ingredients to healing. But prayer will not heal us; God must heal us. He may do so in response to our prayers, but he alone is able to impart the healing touch we so desperately need. God may lead someone else to pray for our healing, but it is God who does the healing. Thus, it is vastly important that we praise and worship him and not the person who is the instrument he may choose to use in our lives.

Christians have debated the issue of healing for centuries. Some believe it is useless to pray for our healing because God has already planned who will be healed and who will not. Others have chosen to follow every so-called "miracle worker" that comes through their town. My own experience has taught me that extreme positions, either way, are usually incorrect. I believe that we can have a balanced view of biblical healing as long as we remember that it is God who does the healing.

FAITH IS VITAL TO OUR HEALING

It is also clear in Scripture that most people were healed in response to their personal faith in God. Believing that God wants to heal us is certainly a vital key to experiencing our healing. Faith is the key that activates our trust in God. Disbelief, cynicism, and doubt will not move the heart of God on our behalf. If we don't believe in his love and grace, we won't believe that he cares enough to hear our prayers. Believing that he really hears us and that he genuinely loves us is crucial to believing that he will heal us. Too many Christians fail to appropriate the healing grace of God because they simply refuse to believe that he can and will help them.

No, we cannot make God heal us. Sometimes, we can believe, confess, and pray and still hear God say, "My grace is sufficient" (2 Corinthians 12:9). Our limited *human* perspective is often inadequate to fully comprehend God's divine plan for our lives. At a given moment in time, we may not be able to see his grand purpose. Like Job, we are left wondering, "Why is this happening to me?" But as time marches on, the greater picture of God's divine purpose is clearly laid out before us.

Faith, not only means believing God for a miracle, it also means continuing to believe even when there is no immediate response. We cannot determine the timetable of God. He alone knows the end from the beginning.

❖

Therefore, God alone knows the proper *timing* for answering our prayers. Our God who created time knows the time and is always on time!

As we conclude this work, I pray that your faith has been strengthened and stretched by our study of the healing touch of Jesus. The same hands that reached out to the poor, the sick, and the needy of the first century reach out to us today in the twenty-first century. The difference is that they are now the nail-scarred hands of the Savior who died on the cross.

After the resurrection, Jesus reached out his hands to the disciples to convince them that he was really alive (see Luke 24:39; John 20:27). When they saw the nail prints, they knew it was really Jesus. Knowing what he has done for us on the cross, we can now see those nail prints by faith. They speak of his love for us and call us to believe in his healing touch—as much today as ever!

MIRACLES RECORDED IN THE GOSPELS

---

1. Cleansing a Leper—Matthew 8:1–4; Mark 1:40–45; Luke 5:12–16.

2. Healing the Centurion's Servant—Matthew 8:5–13; Luke 7:1–10.

3. The Healing of Peter's Mother-in-Law—Matthew 8:14–15; Mark 1:29–31; Luke 4:38–39.

4. Healing the Sick at Evening—Matthew 8:16–17; Mark 1:32–35; Luke 4:40–44.

5. Devils Entering into a Herd of Swine—Matthew 8:28–34; Mark 5:1–20; Luke 8:26–39.

6. Healing the Paralytic—Matthew 9:1–8; Mark 2:1–12; Luke 5:17–26.

❖

7. Raising the Ruler's Daughter from the Dead—Matthew 9:18–19, 23–26; Mark 5:22–24, 35–43; Luke 8:41–42, 49–56.

8. Healing the Hemorrhaging Woman—Matthew 9:20–22; Mark 5:25–34; Luke 8:43–48.

9. Healing the Two Blind Men—Matthew 9:27–31.

10. Healing a Devil-Possessed Dumb Man—Matthew 9:32–34.

11. Healing a Man's Withered Hand—Matthew 12:9–21; Mark 3:1–7; Luke 6:6–11.

12. One Possessed with a Devil, Blind, and Dumb—Matthew 12:22–30; Luke 11:14–26.

13. Healing the Canaanite Woman's Daughter— Matthew 15:21–28; Mark 7:24–30.

14. Healing the Epileptic Boy—Matthew 17:14–21; Mark 9:14–29; Luke 9:37–42.

15. Healing the Two Blind Men—Matthew 20:29–34; Mark 10:46–52; Luke 18:35–43.

16. Casting Out an Unclean Spirit—Mark 1:21–28; Luke 4:31–37.

17. Healing a Deaf and Dumb Man—Mark 7:31–37.

18. Healing the Blind Man at Bethsaida—Mark 8:22–26.

19. The Widow of Nain—Luke 7:11–17.

20. Healing the Infirm, Bowed Woman—Luke 13:10–17.

21. Healing the Man with the Dropsy—Luke 14:1–6.

22. Cleansing the Ten Lepers—Luke 17:11–19.

23. Restoring the Servant's Ear—Luke 22:47–53.

24. Healing the Nobleman's Son—John 4:46–54.

Miracles

Recorded in

the Gospels

❖

NOTES

CHAPTER 3

1. Internet source, used by permission, "Sunday Sermons," Voicing Publications (voicings.com).

2. Joel Gregory, *Growing Pains of the Soul* (Waco, Tex.: Word, 1989), 161.

3. John MacArthur, *The Freedom and Power of Forgiveness* (Wheaton, Ill.: Crossway, 1998), 179–80.

CHAPTER 10

1. Charles Allen, *Life More Abundant* (Westwood, N.J.: Fleming H. Revell, 1957), 15.

2. Lloyd Ogilvie, *Autobiography of God* (Ventura, Calif.: Regal Books, 1979), 12.

3. William Backus, *Telling Yourself the Truth* (Minneapolis: Bethany House, 1987), 29, 31.

CHAPTER 11

1. Charles Allen, *Life More Abundant*, 56.

❖